PATRIOTS WILL

SURVIVING THE GREAT DEPRESSION AND WORLD WAR II COMBAT

A Memoir

Jack C. Hubbard, Major, USAF (RET)

ISBN: 1-4033-5371-9 (e-book)
ISBN: 1-4033-5372-7 (Paperback)

Library of Congress Control Number: 2002093273

This book is printed on acid free paper.

Printed in the United States of America
Bloomington, IN

1stBooks—rev. 10/02/02

DEDICATION

To those who served with the 8th Air Force during World War II

TABLE OF CONTENTS

JUST A SIMPLE SOLDIER

He was getting old,
and his hair was falling fast,
and he sat around telling
his stories of the past.
Of a war that he has fought in
and the deeds that he had done,
In his exploits with buddies;
They were heroes, every one
And though sometimes to his neighbors,
his tales become a joke,
All his buddies listened,
for they knew whereof he spoke.
But we'll hear his tales no longer,
for he has passed away,
and the world's a little poorer,
for a soldier died today.

No, he won't be mourned by many,
just his friends, his kids and wife,
for he lived a very quiet
sort of ordinary life.
He held a job, and raised a family,
quietly going on his way,
and the world won't note his passing;
Though a soldier died today.

When politicians leave this earth,
their bodies lie in state,
While thousand note their passing
and proclaim that they were great.
Papers tell of their life stories
from the time that they were young,
but the passing of a soldier
goes unnoticed and unsung.

Is the greatest contribution
to the welfare of our land,
some jerk who breaks his promises
and cons his fellow man?
Or the ordinary fellow,
who in times of war and strife,
goes off to serve his country
and offers up his life.

The politician's stipend
and the style in which he lives,
are sometimes disproportionate
to the service that he gives
While the ordinary soldier,
who offered up his all,
is paid off with a medal
and perhaps a pension small.

It's so easy to forget them,
for it was so long ago
that the husbands, sons and fathers
went to battle, but we know
it was not the politicians,
with their compromises and ploys,
who won for us the freedom
that out country now enjoys.
Should you find yourself in danger
with your enemies at hand,
would you really want some cop-out
politician with his waffling stand?
Or would you want a soldier
who has sworn to defend
his home, his kin, and country,
and would fight until the end?

He was just a common soldier
and his ranks were growing thin,

but his presence should remind us,
we may need his like again.
For when countries are in conflict,
then we find the soldiers part
is to clean up all the troubles
that the politicians start.
If we cannot do him honor
while he's here to receive the praise,
then at least let's give him homage
at the ending of his days.
Perhaps a simple headline in
the paper that might say:

"Our Country is in Mourning,
for a Soldier Died Today."
(author unknown)

INTRODUCTION

In early 1996 my daughter Cheri asked me to write about my World War II experiences. She was interested in having a written record. I thank her for getting me started on my memoirs. As I wrote this true story I relived these events. The more I wrote the more I could remember. It was amazing the things that popped into my mind that I had not thought about since the war or before. I had almost completed writing my war-time experiences when Cheri asked if I would like to have the letters I wrote to my mother during World War II. I didn't know she had them. I was excited and could hardly wait to receive them! It was so very special for me to read and reread them. They gave me such an added sense of reality I included some of them in this book. Since you will read about my education or lack of, during the Great Depression, I decided not to edit any of the letters. I also did not want to lose the flavor of some of our speech expressions over 50 years ago.

My brother-in-law, Bob McClain, read part of my first draft and suggested I expand it to cover my family history, personal experiences and events prior to the war. My son Scott suggested the title "Will of the Patriots." This I changed to "Patriots Will" because patriots WILL defend our country at all costs so their WILL and legacy will always be a FREE America.

Upon completion, Bunny Goldberg reviewed my manuscript and made some excellent suggestions for improvement, as did Fred Sutton. Thanks to Catherine Pacheco for the outstanding work she did editing my manuscript. Special kudos go to Mary and Jim Tufty for their valuable input. I am most grateful to these dear family members and friends for their interest and contribution. Most of all I thank my wife, Karen. Without her love, support and encouragement, this book would not exist.

1

Since most of our younger generation seem to know little about our history during these precarious times I thought it helpful to insert historical time lines as appropriate, highlighting the sequence of events during the depression and World War II. Hopefully, this will enable them to have a clearer understanding of the wonderful progress our country achieved during those challenging years. I'm privileged to have witnessed them and still marvel at the dramatic events that unfolded. We can never adequately express our gratitude to those people who worked hard to make a dream come true. As beneficiaries of their legacy, I trust we can be worthy recipients and not squander it as we head into the unknown realm of this new millennium.

1. BACK TO BERLIN

Early morning on 8 May 1944, I left the briefing room shaking my head in disbelief! We were scheduled to fly another mission from our base in England to Berlin! I was feeling a little gun-shy at the prospects. This would be my fifth time over the heavily defended Nazi capitol; a dangerous place to be at any time with over 1,600 anti aircraft guns firing away at Allied intruders.

Our group took off with 30 bombers. The problems of flying in poor weather were never better illustrated throughout the history of the 306th Bomb Group than on this day. Five aircraft soon aborted the mission when they were unable to maintain formation while climbing to their briefed altitude. A newcomer to the group, Lt. Darvin Smith, was one of these five. He dropped behind at 9:59 a.m. but later rejoined the formation. He then dropped back another time and was never seen again. It was later learned the entire crew had been killed.

At 10:42 a.m., about one-half hour before reaching Berlin, the single worst tragedy in loss of 306th aircraft not due to enemy action happened. Persistent contrails (vapor trails) made visibility difficult even though it was a brilliant sunny day at this cold and crisp altitude. Lt. Richard Lambert, 369th Bomb Squadron was apparently caught in propeller wash from aircraft in front of him, quickly causing the aircraft to drop on top of another B-17. A rapid sequence of shocking events followed. Lambert's left wing panel flew off and his aircraft seemed to make a loop around the fuselage of the plane piloted by Lt. Edwin Jacobs, 367th Bomb Squadron, completely knocking off the tail section which separated and plummeted in to the wing of a third plane flown by Lt. Edwin Schlect, 369th. We watched in horror as all three aircraft in smoke and flames fell helplessly to their doom. Miraculously four of the 30 crewmembers aboard the three planes survived this awful mid-air collision.

Our whole crew was emotionally shaken after witnessing several catastrophes. But sorrow was immediately replaced with concern for our own survival as we rapidly approached our target. We dropped our bombs at 11:11 a.m. My bombardier sounded that all familiar "Bombs away" over our interphone system. I quickly opened the door from the radio compartment of the bomb bay to see if all of the bombs had actually dropped. To my surprise and dismay, one of the ten 500-pound bombs still hung in the bomb rack that was parallel to the catwalk. It was my duty to kick it out of the airplane! There was no military training manual explaining the procedure for kicking bombs out of a B-17 flying five miles above Mother Earth during such terrifying conditions. Presumably I was expected to depend upon 'Yankee' ingenuity to come to the rescue in such on-the-job training situations.

Leaving the target as soon as possible, my pilot started evasive action attempting to avoid the horrendous amount of flak exploding all around us. I had to act quickly! I grabbed the portable oxygen bottle (aircraft was not pressurized) and started moving toward the bomb. Holding on to metal vertical struts, I inched my way along the narrow catwalk not much wider than my boot. The ground, over 20,000 feet below, was visible through the open bomb bay doors. There was nothing but space on both sides of me. Fortunately, I only had time for a quick look at the ground below. The bitter cold wind whipped through the bomb bay as the swerving, gyrating, unsteady plane continued along its way, unsure of its destiny. The sound of flak shells exploding close by was earsplitting. Steel shrapnel burst in various sized pieces flying in every direction. Some hit our aircraft. It sounded like heavy drops of rain on a tin roof in a bad thunderstorm. They belched huge puffs of black smoke so thick it looked as though you could easily walk on top of them. This was not conducive to my balancing act on the bomb bay catwalk because time was of the essence. Reaching the bomb, I gave it a hard kick. Nothing happened. It didn't budge with the next kick! Ice was forming rapidly on my oxygen mask. I was miserably cold and could feel my strength waning. It was now or never! Mustering my strength for what could be my last effort, I began kicking furiously. Finally, the bomb dropped. Probably in some farmer's field. I scampered back to the radio room and announced on the interphone "Bomb bay all clear."

After stowing the oxygen bottle I returned to my seat. Resting a few minutes to get my breath and warm up, I glanced at the top of my radio receiver in front of me. My eyes settled on my parachute. In my haste to get to the bomb I had forgotten to put it on! Indescribable feelings washed over me, including that of pure terror. I would have perished had I fallen through the bomb bay.

Just after bombing, Lt. Louis Matichka, 367th, left the group in no apparent trouble. He did not return to base. Later we learned he had engine trouble and had to feather #1 engine. Shortly thereafter #4 engine began detonating and vibrating excessively. There was only 500 gallons of gas left. knowing he couldn't make it back to England, Lt. Matichka headed for Sweden. He almost made it. Approaching the coast, he ran out of fuel. He had to ditch the aircraft in the North Sea about one half of a mile from shore. Fortunately it was shallow water. They were interned in neutral Sweden for the remainder of the war. How lucky can you get!

No enemy aircraft attacked our Group but hit those to the left and ahead of us. Our fighter escort support was excellent with no gaps reported. Ack Ack fire was moderate with both barrage and tracking inaccurate. Still, it was a very bad day for the 306th, losing five crews and bombers. The next day, the U.S. military newspaper, Stars and Stripes, headlined "Reich's Skies See Fierce Battles—U. S. Losses 49, Nazis' 110." The article stated

"Thousands of American and Allied planes stormed across Europe yesterday in their incessant campaign to cripple German resistance before the Allied invaders strike and the Red Army launches its final offensive from the east. American heavy bombers, numbering up to 1,000 and escorted by the like number of fighters, battled through furious Nazi fighter resistance to give Berlin its second daylight bombing in 24 hours and to bomb the rail and aircraft manufacturing center of Brunswick," etc.

We returned safely to our base but that sad day will be forever etched in my memory. It was heart breaking losing five crews of brave, courageous young men on one mission. They were the heroes! I was more than happy to have completed my 19th mission without a mishap. Only six more to go and then home! I was a veteran. An old timer. New crews looked up to me with both awe and respect. Mainly because I had completed most of my missions. I reflected on how fortunate I was to still be alive. Then I thought about the horrors of war, wondering, "What am I doing here? What brought me here?" It seemed a long and arduous journey crammed into a few short years of my young life. So much had happened. But you be the judge of "what brought me here" by reliving the same journey with me. Let's begin!

2. IN THE BEGINNING

President George Bush in his presidential campaign of 1992, referred to a "Gentler and Kinder World." As I reflect back on my life, I truly believe I was born into such a world.

My grandfather, Charles Joseph Hubbard of English heritage and a Protestant, was born in Bedford, Ohio, in 1860. His oldest brother served as a Captain in the Union Army during the War Between the States. Grandfather married Anna Dillon, a Catholic from County Roscommon, Ireland. My grandmother, who died before I was born, claimed to be a cousin of Lord Dillon, the Earl of Roscommon. Two of my three aunts, all Catholics, died before I was born. I remember my Aunt May who died when I was about seven years old. My father, Charles Hine Hubbard, was born in Birdseye, Indiana and along with his sisters was raised a Catholic. After attending University of Notre Dame for three years, he renounced Catholicism based on "compulsion of the individual" and resigned from the school. After converting to Protestantism he completed his senior year at Columbia University. My father then followed my grandfather's footsteps and became a Mason and a Knights Templar.

I was born in Huntingburg, Indiana, on 25 March 1922. I was named after my father, Charles Hine Hubbard, Jr. As a small child I was called Junior, which soon became Jackie. I later changed my name to Jack Charles Hubbard. Sadly, my parents didn't have a happy marriage. They divorced when I was three years old and my father was awarded custody of me. I never learned why. When I turned five my father and grandfather, who were quite wealthy, moved to Spartanburg, South Carolina where they built and operated a barrel stave factory.

October 1929—The Stock Market crashes with huge investor losses. Many banks and businesses failed. The Great Depression followed with millions of people out of work. No government programs were available to assist these people who had to depend upon families, friends and churches to help them through the hard times. Many survived with their dignity intact without government handouts.

Spartanburg was a small, sleepy college town with a population of about 28,000. They were 'salt of the earth' folks, people who made this country great. They were good Christian, law-abiding citizens who genuinely cared for each other. It was a time when people left their homes and cars unlocked and welcomed a new neighbor with a special pie or cake. Businesses closed by 1:00 p.m. on Saturday and didn't reopen until Monday morning. People worshipped God, spent time with their families, and rested on Sundays. A drug store was open for emergency prescriptions. One of the few restaurants in town and a couple of service stations would also be open.

The area's primary industry was cotton with seven mills supporting hundreds of people. Spartanburg was noted for its Elberta peaches, some of the best anywhere. In those days wild delicious blackberries grew in abundance along the roadside. They were available to anyone. We often picked them off the bushes. Most roads were unpaved between towns. It didn't matter much because there weren't many cars in existence in the late twenties and early thirties. There was little if any pollution; the rivers and creeks were clean. Some streams were so crystal clear you could see all the way to the bottom. People would often drink the water. I remember how beautiful they were with fish swimming over multi-colored rocks and lush vegetation growing along the banks.

1932—Franklin D. Roosevelt became President of the U.S.

1933—Adolph Hitler became Chancellor of Germany.

For six years I walked about a mile to Southside Grammar School. The school building is gone. I carried my books in one hand and my lunch in a brown paper bag in the other. We didn't have a cafeteria. In those days we went to school to learn and accepted silence as the standard in the classroom. We were taught manners and respected other people's rights. Most realized the importance of discipline and consideration of their fellow classmates. The teachers would not tolerate bad behavior or not paying attention in the classroom. If we wanted to speak, we had to hold up our right hand and be recognized by our teacher. Anyone misbehaving would have to stay after school, often for several days. Male students who did not obey the teacher were sent to the school principal. No one ever wanted that experience. Mr. Patton, a big man, weighed about 250 pounds. I never knew anyone who went to this office a second time; the first was always sufficient. He would take off his long black belt and give the offender a few light strokes on their buttock. The student was given a note to take home to his parents, explaining his particular breach of discipline. The parents usually gave their child another licking, often worse. I know all of this from a one-time, first-hand experience.

Mr. Patton was truly a congenial, caring and lovable gentleman, admired and respected by all who knew him. The school had no other auxiliary staff; administrators, counselors, teachers' aides and such. Today it seems all these others outnumber teachers, who should be primary. When we finished our grammar school we could at least read, write, and solve arithmetic problems. If a student failed they were required to repeat that year's work. Few failed because most kids were naturally competitive and wanted to succeed. Since then it seems we've gradually lost our way. We are now graduating young people who are not prepared academically to cope with the realities of life.

I still remember two teachers who helped mold my young life for the better: my third grade teacher, Mrs. Irwin, and Mrs. Steele, fifth grade. The school had few outside activities but we always had an annual walk to the Confederate Soldiers Monument near our school. We were joined by elderly veterans whose Confederate uniforms were resplendent with medals. Sadly, with each passing year their numbers diminished. I was impressed and happy to see these old soldiers being honored. During my military years I sometimes thought about those days of innocence.

After school we rode our bikes or roller-skated. We played hockey often in the street using broom handles as hockey sticks and crushed tin cans as pucks. Sometimes we played various games of marbles. I still have the marbles I played with as a kid so I can now honestly say, "I haven't lost my marbles"—and prove it.

Saturday was a big day for kids in Spartanburg. I attended the Montgomery Theater on North Church Street to see a movie and vaudeville show. It was the beginning of my love for popular music. I first heard what was to become my favorite song, Duke Ellington's "Sophisticated Lady". Other times I would go to the Strand Theatre on Main Street and see two cowboy movies and a serial for ten cents. I'd arm myself with a big bag of popcorn for only five cents and have the time of my life. I loved to see those old 'shoot'em up Bill movies with Ken Maynard, Tom Mix, Bob Steele, Hoot Gibson and other cowboys...heroes of the action films of the day. Sometimes on the way home I would stop at a tiny greasy spoon restaurant, just a hole in the wall. For a nickel they served the best hotdog I ever ate. I can still taste the succulent pure beef and smell the mouth-watering aroma of onions, mustard, and relish.

A haircut cost just ten cents. Ah yes, how cheap living was then. Baby Ruth, Butterfinger and similar candy bars sold for four cents each or three for a dime. Coffee was five cents with as many refills as you desired. A good plate lunch was only twenty-five cents. It was said a man making two hundred dollars a month had it made financially. That became my goal in life. How quickly times changed. As a youngster, I earned a little money selling figs in season. Our neighbor's fig tree branches arched over into our backyard. I made sure my neighbors didn't see me when I cautiously picked figs from his tree. As I peddled them from house to house, I wondered if we had air rights to the figs.

I also sold magazines such as Ladies Home Journal, Grit, and Liberty from door to door. Before I left Spartanburg I was a carhop at the La Petite Elite Drive In Restaurant near Converse College, a school for women.

Giving Wofford College, a men's school, equal time, I sold cold drinks at home games during football season. This was my initial training as a salesman. I believe it helped me in later years. Eventually I became a top salesman in the life insurance and later the mutual fund companies I represented.

My father moved to Spartanburg because there was an abundance of white oak timber in South Carolina. The wood was used in the manufacture of staves, the curved wooden sections of a barrel. Whiskey and wine barrels were primarily exported to Europe. Prohibition was in effect in the U.S. at that time. Later it was repealed and the company also made beer barrel staves for use in the U.S. The Carolina Stave Company was a successful business until the depression in the 1930's.

I remember traveling around South Carolina with my father during the summers. There was no air conditioning in cars or anywhere else for that matter. It was stifling hot at times. Few roads were paved so dust blew everywhere. My father bought white oak timber and had crews of men cut down the trees, saw them into logs and then cut them into their required lengths. For example, some were fifty-four inches long, which were further split into a pie shaped piece measuring perhaps two inches by one inch when looking at them vertically from the topside. My father and the foremen graded each stave by marking one end with a color code indicating the quality before shipping them. The many varied qualities of staves were segregated into different stacks for identification prior to shipment. I recall seeing as many as eight or ten boxcars loaded with staves. They would sit on the railroad siding before being hauled by freight train to the Carolina Stave Company in Spartanburg. There they would be sawed into barrel sized staves and stacked outside the plant to dry out completely before being shipped to various locations in Europe and South Africa.

3. THE GOOD OLD DAYS

Around 1930, my father developed a romantic interest in three ladies, each living in different places. My father and I eventually visited each of them at their homes in Louisville, Kentucky; Miami, Florida; and Woodruff, South Carolina. He asked me which one I liked best. My favorite was Lillian and since she was his choice too, he married her. She was the one from Kentucky; an elegant widow lady whose deceased husband had been a prominent attorney. Here sister, Edith, was married to Leslie Howard, (not of Hollywood fame). They had a lovely daughter, Virginia, who was two years older than me. We became lifelong friends and she eventually became a gifted professional musician leading her all girls orchestra during the 1940's. Later, as an accomplished pianist, Virginia played the chic nightclub circuit in New York and Florida. Lillian was a very good mother to me. I loved her very much.

My father had a Packard limousine driven by a liveried chauffeur. Sometimes he drove us to visit our closest friends, the Daniels, Elmer and Emma. To me they were Uncle El and Aunt Em. They always had a fresh pot of coffee for my father when we made our daily mid-morning visit. Everyone seemed to have enjoyed this time of fellowship together. They would also play bridge once or twice a week. My father taught me how to play and when I was about twelve years old I could play a hand or two with the 'big folks'. Later in life I became an excellent player and participated in duplicate bridge tournaments. Soon after turning twelve years old I became a Boy Scout, which I thoroughly enjoyed. This was a wonderful time in my life. I loved the overnight camping in beautiful heavily grown woods where we cooked our own meals over an open campfire. I recall eating roasted potatoes, black on the outside and almost raw on the inside. I totally enjoyed the burned hotdogs

13

and marshmallows. I read a lot. My favorite books were the Tom Swift series and others like them.

We visited the Daniels several nights a week for dessert and coffee and listened to our favorite radio programs: Jack Benny, Fred Allen, Amos and Andy, Eddie Cantor, Lum and Abner and others. All broadcasts were in AM (Amplitude Modulation). Radio receivers operated on vacuum tubes. We received major programs primarily from the two high-powered stations in the Eastern part of the United States, WLW in Cincinnati, Ohio and KDKA in Pittsburgh, Pennsylvania. At that time, all station call signs east of the Mississippi River started with W except for Pittsburgh, and west of the Mississippi they all began with a K. Even though these were high-powered stations, our reception would sometimes have static and the signal would fade in and out. We would listen to Kate Smith on WBT, Charlotte, North Carolina, and the limited programming on our local station WSPA in Spartanburg. In those early days of radio there weren't very many stations and the national networks were just coming into existence. Few people had radios back then.

I'll never forget Julia May Turner, the young black lady who worked for us in Spartanburg. After six years, the time came when we couldn't afford to pay her but we still tried to share what we had with her. She was like a member of our family; she loved us and the feeling was mutual. Julia May had a wonderful sense of humor. My daddy kidded a lot and she would laugh uncontrollably as tears ran down her face. It was a different kind of world then between blacks and whites. My parents and I attended Bethel Methodist Church occasionally. When they didn't attend, I went with some of my neighbors. My best friend, Jesse Trott, was a member of a Southern Baptist Church. He invited me to attend church with him. I really liked it and when I was twelve years old I received Jesus Christ as my personal savior.

Although my father read and studied the Bible he was also interested in Astrology, Rosicrucian's and Eastern religions. His friends called him "Bood" for Buddha. Today he would be called a "New Ager". The American Astrology magazine published some of his articles. He was considered by his peers to be proficient preparing personal horoscopes and giving readings. Later, while living in Hollywood, California, he occasionally earned money that way. He once worked at Newberry's Five and Ten Cents store on Hollywood Boulevard giving psychic readings and selling horoscopes. I used to call them 'horrorscopes'. He wore a red fez (similar to that worn by a Shriner) and sold various astrology information. As a child there were times I thought my father was 'far out'. Even so, I never doubted he dearly loved me and wanted only the best for me. He was the first to help the needy, sometimes to his own financial detriment. I remember him as a kind, gentle and compassionate man who often bought food and coal for families in need. During the Depression he continued to pay all of his employees at the stave factory every week, expecting the Depression to end at any time. Unfortunately weeks became months but he still kept them on the payroll as long as he could.

My father played the piano beautifully even though he never had a lesson. This was not my forte' but he always encouraged me in sports. As a youth I was an excellent baseball player and suffered only a few broken fingers. I was a long ball hitter. My father and others called me "Home Run Jackie". There was no such thing as organized baseball for youngsters. The American Legion had a small-scale annual competition. No Little Leagues. No playing fields. We played in a vacant lot carefully dodging trees and such. Occasionally we would blast a ball far enough to break windowpanes in someone's house. When that happened we scattered at a gallop in every direction hoping no one saw who did it. None of us could afford to replace windowpanes and most of our parents couldn't either. I didn't do well in football and got banged up a few times. We wore only small shoulder pads and a leather helmet without a face guard or other protection. I eventually got tired of cuts, bruises and a bloody nose and quit playing. The way we played then reminds me of the way Australian Rules football is now played. I retained the love of both baseball and music throughout my life.

4. TOUGH TIMES

My grandfather was in great physical shape at age seventy-four in 1934. How ironic he was killed in front of our house by a drunk driver. He was very special and I loved him very much. He was an elegant looking gentleman, and dapper in dress. Pop, as I always called him, was highly respected in the community. He had the reputation as an honorable and astute businessman. Truly "Mr. Carolina Stave Company". Every Sunday he gave me a nickel. It would buy a whopping amount of candy in those days. I was mystified when he reached into his pocket of change and pulled out the lone five-cent coin. As a little kid, I wondered how he could pick out my 'Sunday Nickel' out of all his change. When I misbehaved and a spanking was deserved, Pop would instead pick me up and shake the living daylights out of me. I much preferred a spanking by my father. My grandfather taught me if anything is worth doing, do it right. Most of all, that stuck with me all my life. No matter what the job, I would go all out to do it to the very best of my ability. It didn't matter whether it was mopping floors, selling or soldiering.

My grandfather's death was a great shock to everyone, especially my father who had depended upon Pop's leadership and guidance in the business. It seemed everything went downhill from that point on. In order to live, my father eventually sold all our family belongings, piece by piece, including his once expensive beautiful three-carat diamond ring. The $50.00 he received for it was a fortune. Times were difficult. Most people called the depression "hard times". Often for lunch I had a sandwich of white bread with tomato ketchup or mayonnaise for the filling. Meager though these sandwiches were, I liked them. Occasionally, I enjoyed the treat of having a sandwich with sliced onions, mayonnaise, salt and pepper. Most of the time, fresh

17

vegetables were fairly cheap in the markets, so we usually fared better at dinner.

1935—Mussolini, Fascist leader of Italy, ordered the invasion of Abyssinia (Ethiopia) in Africa

---

My father drank heavily for several years as his addiction grew. He could not accept losing his father, his business, and the family breakup.

In 1935, in frustration, my stepmother went to live with her niece, Virginia in Louisville, Kentucky. Alone now, my Father and I hitchhiked to Hollywood, California. We had a total of $5.20 when we left Spartanburg. Automobile rides were easy to get during those hard times. People trusted each other and crime was almost unheard of. Most people suffered through really tough times. But still, there was a spirit of kindness and a tendency to help each other; social welfare had not yet arrived on the scene. People who provided transportation would occasionally buy us a meal or give us some change, even a dollar, once in a while. Most people were happy to share what they had.

It took about a week to reach California. I was impressed with the beauty and vastness of our great country. I remember my first crossing of the Mississippi River. It brought back memories of Tom Sawyer and Huckleberry Finn from Mark Twain's wonderful books. I was around thirteen years old and had a vivid imagination for my age. I thought we would never get through Texas...it was so big. Oil wells seemed to be pumping liquid gold in rhythm with each other. Real cowboys were new and exciting to me, especially after seeing my heroes portraying them on the silver screen. I discovered the stars really were big and bright in Texas. I still get that certain glowing feeling when I think about Texas...a feeling one has to experience to comprehend.

It was quite another experience to cross the desert and see beautiful scenery in Arizona and New Mexico. The characters in Zane Grey's book, "The Riders of the Purple Sage" seemed to come to life. It looked as though an artist had painted that magnificent scene as the entire horizon came alive in an array of color. When we arrived in Los Angeles we went to the Union Rescue Mission at Fifth and Main streets. We were treated kindly by folks there who provided us with soup and bread for the stomach, a short sermon for the soul and a clean bed for a night's sleep.

5. BACK AND FORTH

After a few months of difficult times in Hollywood, my father contacted my mother. He asked if I could live with her. She happily said yes. Mother had remarried and had another son, Pat. I went to Chattanooga, Tennessee, and moved in with my mother, her husband Ed, and my half-brother. I was now about fourteen and had almost no prior contact with my mother. About three years previously she came to Spartanburg and I talked to her for a couple of hours. She was a total stranger to me. I didn't know her and this caused a lot of problems. I was eight years older than my little brother but we hit it off very well. I always loved him as though he were my real brother. It grieved me deeply when we lost him to brain cancer as a young adult. My stepfather, thirteen years older than my mother was good to me. I always felt it was gracious of him to accept me into his home. He had not finished high school but became a Master Mechanic making a decent living until the depression. During the depression, like many, he was forced to accept work at a considerably lower salary.

My mother's family was from Pennington Gap, Virginia. She was the youngest of twelve children and a college graduate, which wasn't the norm in those days. During the Civil War her father, Marion Parsons, went to Kentucky and joined the Union Army because he did not believe in slavery. This was a brave move as Virginia was a Confederate state and Virginians were not sympathetic to those who did not believe in their cause. My mother was a devout Christian who attended church regularly. For over forty years she belonged to the same Sunday school class. She studied her Bible daily and was an avid reader. This often created a cultural vacuum between her and my stepfather. She was always well versed in current events and liked to discuss them with me throughout her life. Though not always in good health, she was a salesperson at J.C. Penney so she could help my brother, Pat, with his college expenses. Unfortunately, she experienced a lot of sickness and had several major operations.

I attended Dickinson Junior High School in Chattanooga. The ninth grade was a difficult year for me, especially trying to learn Latin and algebra. I earned money delivering The Chattanooga Times on an early morning paper route before daylight. My route had a large number of black families. Saturday was collection day. Everyone was nice and treated me kindly. Occasionally I was invited inside a home but most of the time my customers paid me at the door. I got along with the black people as well as the whites, sometimes better. There was a bakery in the area and I could smell the goodies baking a block away. As I came closer the aroma was irresistible. I always stopped and had several oven-fresh doughnuts, cinnamon buns, or other treats that seemed to melt in my mouth. Over the years, I haven't found any that tastes that good. The paper recognized me on several occasions as carrier of the month because of my dependability and ability to add new subscribers to my route.

Over the next four or five years I bounced back and forth between my father and mother. I was fourteen years old during my first stay in Chattanooga. I missed my father and wanted to be with him so I ran away from home. I hitchhiked to California and made the journey in a little over a week. But it was not without some interesting experiences. I caught a ride out of Big Springs, Texas in an old Ford. Two guys in blue pants and shirts picked me up just as dusk was setting in. They were rough looking characters. One of them asked me if I had any money. I said "no", which was not uncommon during those Depression days. Actually, I did have a few dollars but hoped they wouldn't search me. After a while they told me they had just escaped from prison. I was scared almost speechless wondering what they were going to do. As night wore on, the gas tank showed almost empty. Since they had no money, one of the fellows said we'd have to siphon gas from a car. They used a large empty can and a small rubber hose to siphon gas from a car parked on a deserted street. After taking turns siphoning, one of them told me it was my turn. Having no previous experience, I quickly learned from my qualified instructors...the prison escapees. This was a terrible experience. I got gas in my mouth and on my face and clothes. The fumes were overpowering. I hoped no one would light a cigarette and blow us to kingdom come.

Again, my vivid imagination ran wild! Why were these guys in jail? Were they killers? What were they going to do with me? I was afraid to ask questions! I prayed they wouldn't hurt me. It seemed we weren't making much progress as we traveled down the highway. The hours seemed to pass like days. I thought tomorrow would never come. As the sun peeped up over the horizon, we arrived in Pecos. I was so happy to see daylight knowing the long, nerve-wracking night had finally ended. The one who seemed to be the leader ordered me out of the car. He told me in no uncertain terms to get on my way to El Paso. He added that I'd better not say anything about them to anyone or he would come after me and "do me in". I thought I'd had a nightmare and was sure no one wanted to hear about it. Having been half frightened out of my wits they sure didn't need to worry about my squealing on them. I couldn't wait to hotfoot it out of Pecos. I immediately started walking briskly out of town trying to thumb a ride as quickly as I could.

I got a ride from Pecos to El Paso without difficulty. But then I tried for two days to thumb a ride out of El Paso with no luck. There was hardly any automobile traffic. I had slept under a billboard sign for two nights and was anxious to be on my way to California. I was hungry and went to a Catholic Church and asked for food. They gave me several ripe bananas that took the edge off my teen-aged appetite. The railroad tracks ran through downtown El Paso. I thought maybe I should ride the rails to California since I hadn't been successful in getting a lift by car. Freight trains never appealed to me; I thought it was dangerous getting on and off while they were in motion but by now I was getting anxious to move on. I met a hobo whose appearance looked like he spent his life traveling on freight trains. He was full of information and ready to give advice to anyone who would listen. Mr. Hobo told me to walk eastward along the tracks and look for an empty boxcar being assembled as part of a train enroute to Los Angeles. He said when I got to the railroad yards, ask someone to identify the cars going to L. A. so I would be on the right train. He told me to be on the lookout for 'Texas Slim', the railroad detective who had a notorious reputation for apprehending anyone trying to steal a ride. Apparently, Texas Slim didn't have much regard for the methods he used, including use of a Billy club. Another man showed me empty cars scheduled to go to Los Angeles. He too warned me about Texas Slim.

I climbed through the empty boxcar door and tried to close it along with the door on the opposite side. Neither would close completely. I thought my best chance to remain undetected was to go to one end of the car and hide in the corner where it was almost dark. I knew the train was scheduled to pull out in about half an hour. As minutes ticked away I became more confident I would be on my way without making the acquaintance of the infamous Texas Slim. Suddenly one of the doors flew open. A flashlight caught me in its beam. A deep, strong voice bellowed, "This is the law, come out now!" I shot up like a rocket toward one door as Texas Slim was climbing through the other. Everything was a blur, happening so quickly. I barely made it out of the car ahead of him. I ran all the way back into town. Luckily, I was young and could outrun him.

I waited for a train to come through town, hoping I'd find a car I could board. A few minutes later a freight train came into view; fortunately for me it was chugging along at a slow speed. I watched the loaded boxcars, one by one; creep by at a snail's pace. Many cars went by and it appeared there were no empty ones of any kind. Soon the caboose came into sight a few hundred yards away. My hopes of leaving El Paso quickly diminished. I felt very discouraged. Suddenly an open gondola car came into view. It looked empty. I realized it was now or never. I ran along the side of it, climbed the short ladder, pulled myself over the side, and dropped a few short feet onto sand.

The gondola was only partially filled with sand. Much to my surprise it was crowded with people. Maybe forty. I sat in the sole spot available, with a black couple on one side of me and an older man on the other. As we crossed the desert that night I thought I would freeze. It was terribly cold. I began to tremble as the chilling wind whipped around the inside of the gondola. As the sun finally came up it didn't take long for the heat to become almost unbearable. The sand seemed to reach almost scorching temperatures. It felt like I was in a frying pan. The friendly black couple had a gallon jug of water. They shared it with me and it was a lifesaver! Few people had water and many had a rough time, especially during the hottest part of the day. Our train stopped now and then to pick up water for the engine or let a fast train go by. At one stop, a tramp coming from Los Angeles told us not to go into the city because the police arrested everyone they caught. Most were returned to the Arizona border. California was overwhelmed with people from many states who were jobless and down and out. They suffered abject poverty with no one to turn to. Not even their government. There was no such thing as federal or state assistance. These poor souls were depicted in John Steinbeck's, The Grapes of Wrath, a best seller about the Okies (people from Oklahoma). Okies and other folks left their mid-west farms and ranches in droves. Their property became dust bowls due to several years of severe drought. Nothing would grow. They departed with whatever they could carry, either on foot or by car. Most of these people headed for California, the Promised Land, hoping for a better life and future. I was glad to be back in Hollywood but not for long. After a few months I had difficulty coping with my father's drinking habits and his inability to get and hold a job. I voluntarily returned to Chattanooga, hoping this time everything would work out for the better.

1938—The German Army occupies their neighbor, Austria, who virtually surrendered without a struggle.

---

6. CUTTING THE APRON STRINGS

About a year later things were not working out for me in Chattanooga so I decided to return to my father in Hollywood. Once again I tried to hitch a ride out of El Paso, my previous nemesis, and, bingo, I hit the jackpot! Standing along the highway for just a short time, I was picked up by a guy in a new Cord car. What a snazzy automobile! It was bright yellow with beautiful leather interior. It had several shiny, round, silver-looking supercharged pipes coming out of each side of the motor. This dream car was so streamlined it looked like it was moving while standing still. I told him Los Angeles was my destination and he said he was going home to Hollywood. Good Fortune smiled on me once again. I became excited and told him I was going to my father in Hollywood. This man seemed to be in a hurry or liked to drive fast. There was no time wasted getting to Hollywood. He dropped me off at my father's doorstep, only a few blocks out of his way. This was another of my incredible experiences. Was this the luck of the draw or was it my Guardian Angel looking out for me? I have to believer the latter!

I started selling newspapers at night at the intersection of Sunset Boulevard and Vine Street in Hollywood. I enjoyed it as I wove my way through traffic but it was a rather dangerous way to earn money. My father and I rented a room and shared a bath at a private home on McFadden Place in Hollywood. I attended nearby Hollywood High School for a while. Judy Garland was in my history class but she missed most of her classes. She was tutored at the movie studio when she was making a film. The few times I saw her, she looked and acted like the rest of us young people except she was far more effervescent and gregarious. I don't believe any of us, especially at our young and tender ages, including Judy, realized her truly great talent.

While living in Hollywood I later sold newspapers on the corner of Hollywood Boulevard and Vine Street where the Broadway-Hollywood Department Store was located. My father never had a regular job but earned money occasionally writing articles for astrology periodicals and preparing horoscopes for people. I worked from noon until 6:00 p.m. and earned about fifteen dollars a week. Our room rent was five dollars a week, food was five and the remaining five was spent for incidentals. We frequently ate at Simon's Cafeteria on Hollywood Boulevard for 15 cents each. I loved the movies and attended Graumanns Chinese and Egyptian Theaters and Lloyd Pantages on a regular basis. My father and I enjoyed evening walks, sometimes as far as Beverly Hills. One of my favorite pastimes was riding the open-top, double-decker buses from downtown Los Angeles to Hollywood along Sunset Boulevard. There was no pollution, making it an especially beautiful place then. It was a memorable experience to ride under the stars and enjoy the sights along the way. I also liked to ride the Pacific Electric Company's big red streetcars down the middle of Hollywood Boulevard on the trip from Los Angeles to Santa Monica. It was quite inexpensive. I believe the fare was ten cents one way.

I often saw radio and movie stars driving by or walking on the sidewalk. Some bought my newspapers and sometime they would chat with me briefly. Occasionally when I left my corner spot, people would pick up a paper and leave money in my cigar box. No one ever stole any money. I saw Mae West, Alice Faye, Jackie Coogan, Edgar Bergen, Jack Benny, George Burns, Maxie Rosenbloom (the boxer), Ann Sheridan, Sydney Blackmer, and others. I regularly attended the free network radio broadcasts at the theaters on Vine Street near Hollywood Boulevard featuring Al Jolson, Martha Ray, Eddie Cantor, Bob Hope, Joe Penner, and programs such as the Lux Theatre, the Jack Oakie Show and a host of others.

Sometimes I caddied on weekends at Lakeside Golf and Country Club. A few of the members were Bing Crosby, Bob Hope, Oliver Hardy, Johnny Weismuller (Tarzan in the movies), James Wong Howe, the famous movie cameraman, Jimmy Fiddler, the leading movie/radio gossiper and many others. Once in a while, these people would give me a ride back to Hollywood. I occasionally caddied at the Riviera County Club. I usually saw Jack Benny and George Burns playing cards in the clubhouse. Several mornings a week I mopped floors and washed windows at a dry cleaners just off Hollywood Boulevard. I never liked mopping floors but I gave it my best shot. The owner was a good boss and also played bit parts in the movies.

At age fifteen I made another trip back to Tennessee to live with my mother. This time I decided to travel a different route and see more of this wonderful land of ours. I planned to go to Salt Lake City, Utah; Cheyenne, Wyoming; and Kansas City and St. Louis before ending up in Chattanooga. I hitchhiked from Hollywood to Salt Lake City with no problems. I walked a short distance out of town and came to a farm. To conserve my meager resources, I asked the farmer if I could do some work for my lunch. He agreed and I pitched hay for a couple of hours. Luckily, as I started to get blisters on my hands, he called me to his home for lunch.

After a feast of delicious home-cooked food, I caught a ride to Green River, Wyoming, which was literally out in nowhere. The railroad was looking for people to work on the tracks, removing old railroad ties and replacing them with new ones. A person who did this was commonly known as a 'gandy dancer', which really means a laborer in a railroad section gang. I was hired on a weekly basis and learned all too quickly that we worked on a quota basis. In other words, we were required to pick up and lay down a number of ties in a prescribed period of time. This made pitching hay look like a vacation! It was the epitome of difficult, manual labor! I never worked so hard before or since. I concluded I'd somehow find a way in the future to use my brain and not my brawn. We slept and ate in special railroad cars on an adjacent siding. As soon as I got my first week's pay, I quit. Trains stopped at our siding to pick up water. In a few hours one stopped. There were no empty boxcars. I had no choice but to climb to the top of one and wrap my belt around the catwalk to make sure I didn't fall off. Believe me, this was doing it the hard way! I put a handkerchief around my face knowing I would be traveling through several tunnels. As we chugged along through the first tunnel I thought I would never see daylight again. It's impossible to describe the volume of smoke the engine produced accompanied by small cinders that beat down on my head and body. It was difficult to breathe but I survived my ordeal and vowed I'd never ride a freight train again. I never did! Twice was enough.

Less than a year later I returned to my father. I thought perhaps we could make a go of it this time. Though he tried for a short time to stay away from his old demon liquor, he couldn't resist. My father would earn a few dollars then booze it up for a few days. I was embarrassed by this behavior. It was leading to a lifestyle I didn't agree with. I didn't know what to do to remedy the situation, if anything. I felt insecure with no future. Later on I became fed up with his drinking episodes and ran away.

I had never seen the 'City by the Bay' so I left Hollywood and headed for San Francisco. I arrived in Bakersfield after dark with no place to stay. Rumor had it that some jails would let a person spend the night so I went to the local jail. They provided a clean, unlocked cell for the night. I left in the morning thanking them profusely for their hospitality. It wasn't exactly the Ritz Carlton, but sometimes beggars can't be choosers. I was 16 or 17 years old but could pass for a little older.

When I arrived in San Francisco I teamed up with a guy about my age. He suggested we pick up a little money panhandling on Market Street. Begging in different locations didn't provide the anticipated cash. I didn't like begging so gave it up for good. We later agreed to stow away on a ship going to some exciting foreign land. We let our beards grow for several days to look older. After checking the sailing schedule for the vessels in port we decided our best bet was one loaded with iron ore scheduled to leave for China in several hours. Arriving at the loading dock, the ship's hatches were being covered by some of the crew. We walked up the gangplank without being noticed and pitched in with the crew covering the hatches. When the hatches were covered we tried to look inconspicuous by mingling with the crew. Then it happened! A sea-going Texas Slim apprehended us. A man in a black suit, looking like a plain-clothes policeman, asked us for our identification. We quickly realized we weren't taking our slow boat to China. This was just the beginning of our troubles.

Next, we were turned over to the Juvenile Authorities. I don't know what happened to my buddy, but I was taken to a detention camp located at Palos Verdes Estates close to Long Beach. The camp was out in the boondocks. Not a soul within miles. After several weeks detention I was sent to my mother. Some agency paid for my ticket. I was thrilled traveling first class on a real passenger train. I enjoyed my trip immensely. Particularly the magnificent scenery as I crossed my beloved country.

March 1939—Nazis take over Czechoslovakia

1 September 1939—The German Army and Air Force viciously attack Poland who surrenders in less than two months. Germany partitions Poland with Russia

3 September 1939—Great Britain and France declare war on Germany fulfilling their treaty obligations.

In 1939 my father and I joined my stepmother in Louisville, Kentucky. Once again we lived as a family, a fact that I, at the age of 17 fully appreciated. My father had grown up in Louisville and a former classmate was now head of a large coal company in that beautiful city along the Ohio River. My father's friend gave him a job selling coal and staked him to some advance pay against commissions. Times were still hard and there wasn't an abundance of money. Lillian, my stepmother, made beautiful silk ties that I sold for one dollar each to anyone who would listen to my spiel. The economy was in the doldrums. Therefore, my father's sales were few and far between, producing only a small income. Luckily, I got a job as an usher at Loews State Theatre on Fourth Street. This large, beautifully ornate theatre had a huge balcony. The ceiling gave the appearance of being outside under the stars at night. This was not only architecturally unique but was a superbly romantic setting for those in love. The ushers wore uniforms with a tux shirt and black bow tie. It was a real production! After dressing in the locker room, our chief usher marched us to the main lobby. We were inspected, given our aisle assignments then went to our various locations. When replacing another shift it was quite a ritual that people enjoyed watching. I liked working there and one special occasion was the premiere of "One Million Years BC," starring Victor Mature, a local boy who made good in the movies.

I tried making sandwiches during the lunch hour at a deli restaurant across the street from Loews Theatre. It didn't take long to find out I wasn't cut out for this work. I've always preferred eating food to preparing it. I quickly found a better job working as a clerk in a Kroger Grocery store. I did all the back-breaking jobs; carrying one hundred pound bags of potatoes from the store basement to the produce department; stocking the shelves with cans and other goods; and carrying groceries to our customers' homes. I learned a great deal about my job. The manger was fair and taught me a lot about operating a grocery store. For various reasons my father did not succeed at selling coal. In April 1940, once again our family split up. My father and I returned to California and Lillian went to live with her niece, Virginia. I loved my stepmother very much and was deeply saddened when we parted this time. It turned out to be the last time we lived together as a family.

April 1940—The Nazi war machine conquers Denmark and Norway.

May 1940—France, Belgium and the Netherlands fall to the overpowering German onslaught. Over 300,000 British and French troops were evacuated to England from the besieged beaches of Dunkirk, France.

When my father worked, which was seldom, he usually ended up going on a drunk for a few days. He wanted to succeed but apparently was unable to cope after losing everything he had except me. The instability in my life with no firm roots or a decent home life was getting to me. I knew I didn't have the schooling I should have had at my age. At 18 I barely had enough credits for two years of high school. I was well trained in the school of hard knocks and had a lot of street smarts. I learned my lessons well but it didn't prepare me for a lifelong vocation. I realized I was personally responsible for some of the problems I'd encountered along the way. I now decided to go out and try it on my own.

---

10 July 1940—17 September 1940—The Battle of Britain

Hitler had over 100 Army Divisions standing by for Operation Sea Lion, the invasion of England. If the invasion was to be successful the Germans had to control the air space over the English Channel and the coast.

First, the Luftwaffe would launch an air offensive against Britain to secure the skies and secondly, drop paratroopers along the coastline followed by invasion barges. The Luftwaffe attacked British shipping in the southern part of England with varying degrees of intensity. The most critical phase of the air battle occurred when the Germans attacked R.A.F. airfields 35 times between 24 August and 5 September. ReichsMarshal Goering perpetrated an intensive attack against R.A.F. fighter bases with the loss of 562 planes and crews. The R.A.F. lost 219 fighters but saved 132 pilots to fly again. Many of the air battles raged two to four miles over Dover, which was called "Hells Corner". If Goering had continued his attack on airfields he could have established control of the air, which could very well have changed the course of the war. Instead, he felt success was not achieved fast enough so he changed his strategy by attacking London, believing the English people would capitulate. The Battle of Britain was won by the R.A.F. that saved the country by a very close call.

7 September 1940—The Blitz of London began with the first daylight raid with 375 planes. The savage destruction lasted 28 continuous days. Never in the annals of time has such a cowardly deed of warfare been inflicted upon non-combatant women and children on such a grand scale as the London Blitz. On 15 September the Germans attacked London with 500 bombers and fighters. The R.A.F. put every available fighter in the air to meet the onslaught. The air battle was three-dimensional, five to six miles high, 60 miles long and 38 miles broad. There were over 200 dogfights (a fight between two or more fighter planes usually at close quarters) in the first 30 minutes of this spectacular air battle. One hundred eighty-five German planes were shot down representing one-third of the attacking force.

However, some individual bombers broke through the gallant defenders and reached the center of London.

Between 7 September and 5 October 1940 over 50 million tons of bombs were dropped on London killing 7,000 people and wounding 100,000. It was indiscriminate bombing with bombs falling everywhere including Buckingham Palace, St. Paul's Cathedral, Westminster Abbey, East India Docks and other famous landmarks.

During these 28 days the Luftwaffe lost over 900 planes. Reichsmarshal Goering, not being able to withstand these tremendous losses, switched to night-time bombing. The R.A.F. fighters were not well equipped at this time for nighttime operations and thus the only opposition to the attacks was anti-aircraft guns guided by searchlights and barrage balloons. The Women's Royal Air Force (W.R.A.F.) manned these facilities at strategic locations throughout greater London. Only occasionally did bombers crash into the barrage balloons and few were shot down. There was little fire-fighting equipment and insufficient water as block after block became burning infernos raging out of control in 27 districts of London.

The British counter attacked at night with the few bombers the R.A.F. could muster hitting German targets. Reichsmarshal Goering had previously stated the R.A.F. could never bomb Germany because of the Luftwaffe defenses. Hitler was furious because the R.A.F. had done so and he vowed his revenge would be a thousand-fold. On 14 November the Luftwaffe dropped one million pounds of bombs on Coventry and smashed it flat as previously done by the Nazis at Warsaw and Rotterdam. Many of the people killed were buried in a common grave. Since Hitler could not kill the British spirit by bombing them into submission he now tried another garish method to annihilate them. On Christmas Day, 1940, the Luftwaffe attacked London in wave after wave dropping thousands of incendiary bombs hoping to burn them into submission. The firebombs caused 1,500 different sections of the city to burst into flames, causing the greatest fire in recorded history. Water mains were destroyed, creating a further shortage of water to put out the uncontrollable fires that blazed virtually everywhere.

Two thousand three hundred seventy-five German planes and crews were lost during the yearlong attack on England. Thousands of homes were destroyed in London. Forty thousand people were killed and 50,000 seriously wounded. The German invasion never took place. Not one single German soldier set foot on English soil. The U.S. and Allies were given precious time to build up their fighting forces and arsenals for warfare which insured later victories.

I deeply admire the English people for their courage, determination and unflappable attitude to persevere under overwhelming odds until victory was in their grasp. I understand why, during the war, they sang the song "There'll Always Be An England".

7. BECOMING A SOLDIER

In 1940 I tried to enlist in the U. S. Army but was rejected because of flat feet. I tried the Navy with the same results. A few months later I saw the Movietone News at a theater, showing the Nazi Army marching through the Arc de Triumph in Paris. The camera showed the crowds of French people watching in horror as it zeroed in on one man with tears streaming down his face. This scene touched me deeply. I'd recently turned 18 and as a young 'green' kid, I thought the war would soon be over. I wanted to do my part to help these people, both the French and British. I decided to go to Canada and join the Royal Canadian Air Force (R.C.A.F.) because I always wanted to be a pilot.

In less than a week I had hitchhiked to Toronto. The trip from Toronto to Montreal took me along the Saint Lawrence River. It was fall and the vistas and brilliantly colored leaves were magnificent. I went to Montreal to join the R.C.A.F. and learned that they were not taking any more volunteers. The Canadian Armed Forces were all volunteers so I decided to find a unit that would not only accept me but would soon be going overseas. The German Army had been most successful with the Blitzkrieg, (a fast-paced attack using mechanized and tank divisions), especially through the Lowlands and around the Northern end of the Maginot line in France. I decided to find a tank unit that would probably be among the first to ship out overseas and go quickly into combat.

I learned about the Three Rivers Regiment (TRR) and joined the Canadian Army on 5 September 1940. The minimum enlistment age was 21. I lied about my age and was lucky not to have to show any proof because I was only 18. Americans did not swear allegiance to the King of England, thereby retaining their American citizenship. This unit was from Trois Rivieres (Three Rivers), Quebec. It was similar to a U. S. National Guard unit, which was comprised of men from the same general geographical region. TRR is one of the oldest Canadian military units and celebrated its 125th year anniversary in April 1996.

My first assignment was six weeks basic training at Lansdowne Park in the heart of Ottawa, the nation's capital. Ottawa was a very beautiful city with its imposing Parliament Building and other old, quaint buildings. We often marched in the streets and parks and I enjoyed the beauty of the flowers and trees. I soon learned the routine all recruits follow and upon completion of training was posted to my unit.

I became a part of the Three Rivers Regiment (Tank) located at Camp Borden, Ontario, a huge training facility near the town of Barrie. The TRR, commanded by Lt. Col. Jake Vining, was later designated the 12th Army Tank Battalion and was part of the Canadian First Army Tank Brigade, commanded by General Worthington. This brigade also included the 11th Army Tank Battalion from Toronto, Ontario, and the 14th Army Tank Battalion from Calgary, Alberta.

The TRR was comprised of a H.Q. and three squadrons, A, B, and C. Initially the majority of men were mostly of French heritage with French as their first language. The exception was B squadron where most Americans were assigned. The squadron commander was Captain Walker. 'Pappy' Powell was sergeant major and my troop commander was Lt. Ferdinand Major. Some other Americans were Harry Dumontier, Danny O'Brien, 'Tex' Burke, 'Pappy' Warmington, 'Tiny' Wilton, Harry Fowler and Johnny Robeson. There were others whose faces I remember but can't recall their names. 'Pappy' was the moniker for the oldest in our outfit. Most of us were conscientious about serving in the Canadian Army and were anxious to help defeat the Nazi regime. A couple of guys were probably just one jump ahead of the law in the United States. One older man claimed he

deserted the U. S. Navy (submarines) so he could get some action in combat. Approximately 10,000 U. S. citizens served in the Canadian Armed Forces during World War II. They were dedicated and determined to defeat Hitler and his war machine at all costs, including the ultimate sacrifice of their lives. They believed this was a just and honorable cause. I wonder how they would have felt about the Americans who went to Canada to dodge the draft during the Vietnam War?

Life was hard in the Canadian Army and discipline was tough. It wasn't as strict as the British and German so called 'Iron Discipline' but close to it. A typical day in the life of a tank trooper, or soldier, prior to going overseas in early 1941, was a busy one. We were up at the crack of dawn and the entire squadron fell out in formation for roll call. Sometimes a 'short arm' inspection was held to check each mans penis for venereal disease. This was a miserable time! In the winter we continued to have our formations outside in the early morning darkness where sometimes the snow would be almost knee high. The non-commissioned officer in charge would use a flashlight for the roll call, as would the medics whenever they made their unannounced inspections.

After roll call, we cleaned our barracks before tending to ourselves. Following this we once again fell out in formation and marched to the mess hall for breakfast. We couldn't have a leisurely breakfast since we had to hurry back to our barracks, change from fatigues to regular uniforms, and get ready for the daily morning inspection of personnel, equipment and barracks. Each soldier and his equipment had to sparkle.Our mattress, blankets, sheets and pillow had to be rolled up in a prescribed manner and placed at the end of our steel cots. Our equipment had to be stacked up in a specific way with all of the brass shining brightly. The backpack was placed on top of the blanket roll with the gas mask to the left of it and the water canteen to the right. Our helmet was placed on top of the backpack and our web belt with straps was placed in front. Our duffel bag, about the same size as a sailor's, was neatly tucked just behind the bedding and equipment. The duffel bag contained everything we owned, including the rest of our clothing, spare boots, personal belongings, brass cleaner, brushes, shoe polish and other necessities. Most of the time everything shined and was perfectly displayed. There were two good reasons for this. First, we were inspected every day so there wasn't much time for things to get dirty. Secondly, if we didn't pass inspection we could be given extra details to perform or be punished, a great incentive! Almost without exception each man took great pride in looking his best at all times and having spotless equipment.

After inspection we fell out in formation for another roll call and close order drill. We'd march around the area and do various drills such as right turn, left turn, about turn. Next we would attend classes or field training. Over a period of months we developed skills in map reading, camouflage, radio operation, gunnery, driving, maintenance, and other disciplines. We had a break for lunch and our training usually ended about 3:30 to 4:00 p.m. We'd return to our barracks and change clothes once again, this time for PE (Physical Education). We'd fall out in formation, participate in another roll call and march off to the athletic field. We did strenuous calisthenics, which seemed to go on forever followed by various games. Believe me, every man was in tip-top shape physically. Then back to the barracks, clean up, change clothes, and go to the mess hall for the evening meal.

At night we studied our lessons, wrote letters, cleaned equipment, shot the bull with our buddies, or went to the canteen, the recreational center near our barracks. Prior to joining the Canadian Army I had tasted liquor only once and drank beer infrequently. When I went to the canteen most men drank beer and nearly everyone smoked cigarettes. Some gambled while playing cards or craps with dice. In those days I guess it was considered the manly thing to do: smoke, drink, and gamble. As time went by, I suppose to become a 'regular guy', I unfortunately indulged in all three. I recall smoking both Winchester and Player cigarettes and drinking Molson and Labatts beer. Young, green kids always wanted to act like men but it was in combat where they truly became men overnight.

You have heard the phrase, "swear like a trooper". Well, Trooper Hubbard learned to swear both in English and French! As I look back on those years of my life and realize what a life-changing experience it was, it is sad there was no one to mentor me in the spiritual realm of life. Perhaps, I was not aware of nor took advantage of the opportunity, if there was one, to participate in Christian activities that would better mold my life spiritually. I was truly in a minority as a Protestant when by far the majority of men were Roman Catholic by nature of their French heritage. Of course, our chaplain J. L. Wilhelm, was Roman Catholic and a wonderful man of the cloth. He always seemed sensitive to the needs of Protestants and the few Jewish soldiers. He later served as Archbishop of Kingston for 15 years.

A few weeks after arriving everyone participated in a forced route march. We marched mile after mile on a paved road with full battle gear. Vehicles and medics followed along to pick up men who dropped out exhausted or fell by the wayside. Each man put forth his very best to complete what was a brutal test of strength, endurance, and physical stamina. I don't recall how many miles we marched before we completed the objective, whatever it was. Many never made it to the end. As an all-volunteer force, older men were accepted if they could pass the physical examination. Many were not in good shape nor could they compete with the younger men. I was 18 and physically fit. I completed the march and was proud my youth and determination paid off. Fortunately, that was the only forced route march we ever had. I never learned its objective and wasn't sure anyone really knew. In retrospect it could have been an exercise to show each man the importance of being in shape physically. It also demonstrated the men's dependence on each other since eventually they would fight as a team in combat. It was quite an experience, which definitely none of us wanted to repeat.

Camp Borden
December 22, 1940

Dear Mother,

I received your letter and was very glad to hear from you. I'm sorry to hear about Edith passing away. I would like to have Virginia and Lillian's address so I can write to them.

I sincerely appreciate you sending me the cigarettes and cake. I haven't yet received them but should tomorrow or the next day because of so many boys in the camp. I know the cake will be delicious for I've never tasted any of yours that weren't. Lucky Strikes are my favorite brand and it sure will be a treat to smoke them after smoking this hay up here they call tobacco.

I trust you will have a lovely Christmas and the very best of all that the New Year will offer. I will continue by answering your questions in the order that you asked them.

1. The officers have your name, etc., and my will.

2. Speaking of furlough, mine is due March 5, 1941 (6 months from the day of enlistment). The furlough is 14 days. I'm planning on coming home (providing we're not overseas by then) and Pat and I can celebrate our birthdays together.

3. I'll try to make this as clear as possible:

(a) American soldiers up here are not allowed to go back to the States because Canada is at war, which would make them liable to internment.

(b) Those who have lost their citizenship can't anyway but I could for I'm still a U.S citizen. (c) The Canadian government don't want the Americans to go home because they could stay in the States and not return to Canada and the Canadian government could do nothing about getting them back because they are U.S. citizens.

(d) If you take the uniform off or leave Canada, you are a deserter.

Well Mother all of these rules and laws really don't mean much because the States and Canada are so closely related so you can take it for what it's worth. I haven't heard of any of our American boys being interned yet. Several of our boys went to New York City last Friday on their Christmas leave. Our leaves are only 6 days and I'm going to Toronto on the New Year's leave. I was paraded before my Squadron Commanding Officer and he told me the best way to go home on my furlough so I've nothing to worry about getting home except the fact that we may be overseas by then. I hope to see you all in March.

4. No one knows when we're going overseas but the "Big Drive" will be in the spring. So...

5. Our uniform is called "battle dress" and consists of a tunic and pants that looks like a skiing suit (khaki) and khaki anklets, black high top boots and a black beret. The Tank Corps are the only one's that wear beret's in the Canadian Army. We have fatigue suits, mechanic uniforms, 2 pr shoes, socks, overcoat, underwear, overshoes, shirts, sweater, kit bag, pack sack, field equipment, winter hat, and many other pieces of clothing.

6. My favorite cigarette brand is Lucky Strike, Chesterfields second, Camels 3rd and Phillip Morris last.

7. I'll send you a picture of myself as soon as possible and also snapshots of myself and buddies around the camp.

8. We get all the programs from the States on the radio. Have gotten as far south as Atlanta, Charlotte and Louisville.

9.   There are nearly 100 Yankee's out of the 600 fellows in my Regiment.   90% of them from the New England states. Tex, my best friend here is from Texas, another fellow from Missouri and myself are the only Southerners.

10.   The camp is located about 75 miles north of Toronto and about 16 miles from the small town of Barrie.

I will be glad to answer any questions you wish to ask.   I've gained over 10 pounds since I've been in the Army.

Today I was out driving in a large 4 wheeled drive Lorry with two gear shifts, 8 speeds ahead, right hand drive and snub-nosed front.   I like to drive them very much.   I'll continue my Wireless Course starting January 3 when everyone is back from leave.   I was receiving 8 to 9 words a minute when we stopped.   Its just like going to school all over again up here.   We're learning radio talk also in the Wireless Course (Radio Telegraphy as it is properly called).   Learning procedures, sending and receiving, study of batteries, No. 9 & 11 radio sets, theory and electricity such as the study of matter, molecules, atoms, protons, electrons, etc.   Its all very interesting.

I can't think of much else to write about so I close.   Give my regards to my friends if you want to.   Oh I forgot something important, please send me my birth certificate which I must have to get back into the States and also is good to have.

All my love to all.

Your son,

Jack

PS I hadn't mailed your letter so will add a little more. I received your package and thanks a million. The cake is delicious. I'm really enjoying the cigarettes (so are the other boys!) and I really needed the handkerchief.

We had a Turkey dinner (Christmas) today and the Officers treated us all and the Sergeants had to serve us today.

I have received several letters in reply to my cards from several of the boys at Loew's in Louisville. One of the fellows is getting a commission (2nd Lt.) in the U. S. Army and another friend is getting promoted to Technical Sergeant. They are going to Mississippi to train.

What's going on around home now? What has been happening? How has Pat been getting along? Pat would have a great time playing with a pistol we use. He could be Tom Mix or the Lone Ranger with the "45" Colt. They are heavy just to carry around. Are there very many boys in the Army from Chattanooga? Are there many stationed at Fort Oglethorpe? What is the attitude down home about the British winning? Everyone up here knows that we're going to win and its only a matter of time. We're disappointed that the Greeks have beaten the Italians so bad and are about ruining our chances with the Tank Corp of going there.

Today is like a Spring day here. How's the weather in Chattanooga? Just as I was getting ready to seal this letter I got a telegram from a friend of mine here in the Tank Corp. and he's in Newark, NJ. and he said he got across the border O.K. in uniform and everything was fine. So I'm sure I will be home in March. Write soon.
Lots of Love,
Jack

Before the U. S. entered World War II, President Franklin D. Roosevelt persuaded Congress to pass the Lend-Lease Act whereby the U. S. leased 50 World War I destroyers to Great Britain and 50 tanks to Canada. I had the fortune, or misfortune, to train on some of those antiquated tanks built around 1916. They were a pitiful looking mass of six tons of steel and virtually useless but better than nothing I suppose. This vividly demonstrated how totally unprepared the U. S. was for war. At the time Canada had been at war just over a year and they were only a step or two ahead of the U. S. One lesson we Americans should have learned from the unpreparedness of World War II is that peace can only be achieved through strength.

Occasionally we troopers visited the nearby town of Barrie where we looked forward to a good meal. At a servicemen's club I met a pretty girl who lived at Lake Penetanguishene. I visited her once at her home and met her family. We corresponded a few times but because of the distance I didn't see her again. It was wartime and we were not allowed much time away from Camp Borden except on leave or short passes. Gas shortages and restrictions made travel difficult. I visited Toronto for the New Year holiday. We welcomed in 1941 at the then classy Hotel York.I don't recall all the details but a few months after joining the TRR at Camp Borden a very unusual military event took place. One dismal and dreary morning, our entire regiment fell out in formation in front of a stand draped in black. A soldier was about to be drummed out of the service because he was a homosexual. The whole thing was a very solemn affair with various officers and NCO's participating on the stand with the corporal standing at attention. Orders were read, his stripes and insignia were cut from his uniform with the drums rolling. He was truly 'drummed out' of the service. It was impressed upon everyone that the military would not tolerate homosexuals for one minute once they were identified. The Nazis and USSR executed all homosexuals, both civilian and military. The foregoing basically illustrates the worldwide attitude toward homosexuals during that time in our history. During the past fifty plus years society has witnessed a dramatic change in attitude. For example, Sydney, Australia now celebrates the annual Gays and Lesbian Day.

8. GOODBYE'S

On 7 March 1942 I went home to Chattanooga, Tennessee, on a 14-day leave and visited my parents and brother. It was wonderful seeing my family again and a meaningful time for me. I knew this would be the last time I could see them before going overseas. Maybe the last time ever...a morbid thought...nevertheless, a real possibility. Before I left Canada, a rumor was circulating that we would soon be going overseas. I was treated like a celebrity at home since I wore a British uniform and the U. S. not yet at war. I was interviewed on radio and by the press and honored at different events. My bother Pat was eight years younger than I but we were very close and had a great time together. My mother and stepfather were proud of their older son but concerned about his future well being. My mother was a devout Christian, and I'm sure her prayers as did those of many others, helped see me safely through the war.

After returning to Canada my training continued much as before except we now had a dire need to train with modern tanks. There is no substitute for training with the real thing. I learned how to drive in the service, most of the time driving a three-ton truck on ice and snow-covered country roads. Luckily I never had a wreck as I slid and skidded along treacherous roads sometimes with no control of my behemoth vehicle. The man who taught me to drive was named Dobson. I'm surprised I remembered his name since that was over fifty years ago. I've had virtually no information about the TRR people during all these years. Like many military units we had our share of square pegs in round holes. I recall the only trained automotive engineer in the TRR was assigned as a cook. Later, some of the French Canadians were transferred out of the TRR because they couldn't speak English clearly enough for voice radio communications between tanks.

April 1941—The German Army invades and conquers Yugoslavia and Greece.

In the spring of 1942 we learned the TRR was going overseas. Everyone was given a seven-day embarkation leave. Chattanooga was too far to travel for such a short time so I visited New York City. In those days it was easy to travel in the U. S. by hitchhiking, especially in a military uniform. During wartime we were not allowed to wear civilian clothes. It was easy for me to hitch a ride because of the uniqueness of the Canadian uniform, very similar to the British uniforms.

As a young man I was overwhelmed and impressed with the attention I received when I got to New York. Many people wanted to wine and dine me, because I was a soldier. Walking past the famous Astor Hotel, the marquee showed Tommy Dorsey and his Orchestra featuring Frank Sinatra, Jo Stafford and the Pied Pipers appearing on the Astor Roof. I went to the Astor Roof and joined the line waiting for tables. After a few minutes a gentleman came and said Tommy Dorsey would like me to be his guest at his table for the evening. WOW! What a memorable experience enjoying a ringside seat and meeting such greats at Tommy Dorsey, Frank Sinatra and Jo Stafford. While the entertainers performed, I remained at the table. I was in seventh heaven listening to the great music and enjoying Molson's, a Canadian beer that was Tommy's favorite as well as mine. Notes from young ladies who wanted to dance with me soon began arriving at the table. I danced with some sharp looking girls and as the evening wore on, my heart seemed to pump a little bit faster. It became more exciting as the night progressed. I had a fantastic evening!

The next night I visited a well-known supper club featuring one of Britain's top pianists and his orchestra. I was his guest for the evening and had another superb night out. The following night I went to the bar of a popular nightclub on 52nd Street. Two men next to me were talking to each other when one of them spotted my uniform. He spoke to me and introduced himself. "I'm Milton Berle and this is Lyle Talbot." I'd barely heard of Berle but had seen Talbot in movies. They kept buying me drinks. As they were leaving Berle handed me a $20 bill and wished me good luck. Later, I went to the Famous Door Nightclub and got the last seat before the entertainment started. I was fortunate to see a live performance by Art Tatum, a blind pianist, considered the best jazz pianist in the world...some say the greatest pianist who ever lived. What a fantastic show Art put on. When he played no one moved or spoke; all you could hear was his mastery of the keyboard. I will always remember that wonderful evening of music.

On another evening I saw Benny Goodman and his orchestra featuring Peggy Lee. I enjoy music and this was a special treat to see the "King of Swing" in person featuring such great artists as Harry James on trumpet and Gene Krupa on drums. I will never forget how wonderful everyone treated me. New York was a vibrant and exciting city in 1941. I enjoyed walking the streets and gazing at skyscrapers, visiting theaters, taxis whizzing by and seeing the Duke's mixture of people from all over the world. People were friendly. The city was safe and clean. What a contrast to now, over fifty years later! I said farewell to New York and headed back toward Canada stopping in Buffalo, New York, at about 7:00 p.m.

At the Statler Hotel I ran into three Americans serving in the Canadian Army. I joined them as they were going to the Chez Ami, a supper club that had an excellent reputation for good food, shows and dancing. Soon after our arrival the owner stopped by and said everything was on the house for the evening. The food was delicious and we never ran out of drinks. The owner came to our table and visited with us. When the floorshow started, he told each of us to pick out a girl as our date for the evening and she could dance with us between floorshows. The girls were gorgeous and went all out to please us. They were quite successful. A spotlight shone on us as we were introduced by the owner. The club was packed with people and we were given a standing ovation. My date was a 20-year-old beauty from New York City. We clicked from the beginning. It was easy to sense the strong attraction we had for each other. I saw her home and it turned out to be another most memorable and enjoyable night!

9. SHIPPING OUT TO ENGLAND

We continued to train and train and then train some more. We were exhausted. Around the middle of June we were alerted for assignment overseas. Everyone seemed thrilled with the good news. It was finally time to say farewell to Camp Borden as we boarded a troop train for the port city of Halifax, Nova Scotia via Montreal.

On board a train leaving Montreal

June 18, 1941

Dear Mother,

Last night we left Camp Borden and boy am I glad. Thank God we're finally on our way over. Before we left we were all confined to our lines and we were very busy packing and getting ready to move.

I received your air mail letter yesterday and was very glad to hear from you. The pictures are wonderful and thanks a million. All the boys complimented the pictures and they wouldn't believe you were my mother because you were so young looking. They said you were my sister.

Tex, Harry and I have berths together and its really swell we will be together. Today is really beautiful. We're on our way east. Probably we'll be on the train for a couple of more days.

I'm glad to hear that Pat's condition is improving and hope the older he gets that it will soon disappear. I know that everything will work for the best for all of you. I never forget my prayers.

When I get to England I will cable you. Keep writing to same address. Write often for it takes quite a while to get a letter over there. I must be going so "Au-Revoir".

Your Son with Lots of Love,

Jack

P. S. Tell everybody hello for me and any "Bundles for Britain" I and the rest of the fellows could use them, care of me.

Our troop movement was classified. Upon arrival at the port in Halifax we boarded our ship, The Windsor Castle. The ship, built in Scotland in 1922, was named by the Prince of Wales who was the Duke of Windsor. Along with its sister ship, The Arundel Castle, they were the prime liners on Union-Castle's mail run between Southampton, England, and the South African Cape. The Windsor Castle weighed 18,967 gross tons, was 662 feet long, 72 feet wide, had a service speed of 17 knots and carried 870 passengers. We stayed in the harbor a day or so while the four other troop ships were loaded with personnel and equipment. I believe two of the ships were French passenger ships that had been converted to troop ships. One had been the French liner, Liberte.

While waiting to sail we listened to the radio and heard a Nazi broadcaster from Germany named Lord Haw Haw. He said the First Canadian Army Tank Brigade getting ready to sail for Scotland would be sunk by German submarines in the Atlantic. This wasn't exactly comforting news since we were still in the harbor. I found it interesting the Germans knew our plans and often wondered how they learned them. During the war years there was a tremendous campaign to educate everyone on the importance of keeping classified information just that...classified. It seemed everywhere you looked there were signs and posters with slogans such as "The Walls Have Ears" and "Is This Trip Necessary?" Both military and civilians were constantly cautioned about revealing information that could help the enemy.

---

21 June 1941—Hitler launched "Operation Barbarosa" the massive attack against the USSR with three million men and 4,000 tanks.

Our five troopships sailed out of Halifax harbor on 21 June 1941 accompanied by ten U.S. Lend Lease destroyers. All ships adjusted their speed to the slowest ship in the convoy; thus progress was slow. The Windsor Castle was the smallest of the troop ships and many men got seasick during the voyage as the ship rolled from side to side and up and down in the rough seas. We were packed in the ship like sardines in a can. Due to close quarters we probably smelled like it, too. We marched outside on deck and many times lost our footing as the ship lurched in rough seas. The entire ship appeared covered with water as it bobbed around like a cork. Many soldiers wondered if our ship was truly seaworthy.

Fortunately, I never experienced seasickness. Prior to sailing I was told seasickness could be prevented by eating a big meal before departing and continuing to eat a lot during the voyage. It worked for me and has ever since. Somewhere enroute across the Atlantic we picked up the British warships Ramillies, a battleship, and the Repulse, a battle cruiser. These big ships were a great escort to have alongside us for a while. I felt we were less vulnerable to attack with the pride of the British fleet close by. Little did I know. Both were sunk a few months later by Japanese bombers in the Pacific. Later The Windsor Castle was sunk off Gibraltar by a German radio-guided bomb.

I didn't know our position while sailing in the North Atlantic Ocean but suddenly all ships were ordered to stop and stay as quiet as possible; there were German submarines in the area. We were told not to throw anything overboard, to refrain from smoking, and turn off all lights that could be seen by another ship. All I could hear was the ocean water lapping against the hull of our ship. Soon a beautiful ocean fog rolled in across the waves and hid all our ships from prying eyes. It was an eerie feeling experiencing the unnatural silence not knowing what to expect next. Maybe the solitude would be broken by the sudden impact of a Nazi torpedo smashing against the hull of our ship blowing all of us to smithereens! We spent a tormenting night not knowing what fate had in store for us. Suspense continued to build up as the first glint of morning was welcomed with high hopes. At about 11:00 a.m. we were cleared to continue our voyage. We were told the fog and stillness kept the German submarines from finding us. We were a happy bunch of campers. There was a special prayer service thanking the Lord for keeping us safe from danger. Everyone participated! From time to time we looked over the side of our ship and saw debris floating by. These bits and pieces of ships that didn't survive Atlantic crossings were bitter reminders of the brutal cost of war.

We had been at sea 10 days when one clear morning at daybreak we sailed up the River Clyde. What a beautiful sight as the bright glow of the rising sun promised a new day. When we dropped anchor in the harbor at Gourock, Scotland the beauty quickly disappeared in to sheer ugliness. We were surrounded by the hulls and parts of ships peeking out of the water that seemed to beckon us to their fate. They were sunk during the many German air raids. Probably because of the lack of small boats or tenders to take us ashore, we waited aboard our ship for several hours before disembarking. It was easy for me to visualize German bombers flying over the harbor dropping bombs on us before we got off the ship. I could hardly wait to leave that ship graveyard. Finally, a tender rescued me from any more agonizing minutes imagining what could have happened. Fortunately there was no raid. Everyone was thrilled to be on land again.

We spent five days as guest of the Scottish people. Families invited as many soldiers as they could accommodate into their homes and treated us like family members. They happily shared their meager food rations and made us feel right at home. Our arrival must have triggered a time of celebration because the unending supply of Scotch whiskey flowed freely and much partying ensued. We visited Glasgow and did a lot of sightseeing. It didn't get dark until well after midnight because of the wartime double daylight savings time. These people were absolutely wonderful and I will always remember their gracious hospitality! We'd learned the Germans bombed the harbor and surrounding area frequently at night and considered ourselves lucky not to witness an air raid while in Scotland.

10. TANKS FOR THE MEMORY

We said farewell to our new Scottish friends and boarded a troop train for England. The all night trip was uneventful. We arrived at West Lavington Downs train station in the southern part of England. We went by truck to our final destination, Salisbury Plains. I wish I could adequately describe our new home. It was like a bad dream, truly the pits, literally in the middle of nowhere. It was tent city! Everything was tents. Tents of all sizes. Most of us lived four or five men in a so-called 'bell' tent. The tent was round and about six to eight feet in diameter with wood floorboards. We could hardly fit into it with all our gear. It was a long walk to the personal bathing and toilet facilities. It's difficult to describe the set-up. Out in the open were about twelve cold-water spigots located at the back of a long wooden counter with space for twelve washbasins. There was no hot water. Each morning we took our shaving gear and walked to our truly 'air conditioned' lavatories. We shaved with cold water and used a three by four-inch steel mirror. It fogged up so badly you could hardly see yourself. We were permitted to take a bath once a week. Our toilets were similar to the old time outhouse; cold, windy and not much privacy. The men assigned to clean out the human waste buckets were called 'honey dippers'. Luckily, I never received this delightful work detail. During the well-known English fog there were some mornings it was difficult to find the latrines. Here's the real zinger; when it rained the whole place was a quagmire; mud, mud and more mud! Believe it or not it once rained almost steadily for over forty days. That's four zero days and nights! The wind made it difficult to keep the rain out of our tents because they were located on a small slope. Thinking back on this now, I can hardly believe it really happened. I wonder how all of us survived! We were young and must have been tough because few of us ever got sick due to the hardship of bad weather.

When we arrived at Salisbury Plains there was little food to eat. As I recall, we had soup, bread, jam and tea but not much else. Hardly enough to nourish or satisfy a group of men. There was a SNAFU somewhere but we never learned what caused the food shortage. Finally, on the third day, we went out en masse on the downs and killed rabbits and picked mushrooms. The mushroom pickers lined up abreast filling their berets as they walked. The rabbit brigade put a hose extension on the back of a vehicle exhaust pipe and blew the fumes in to the rabbit hole killing them with a shovel as they came out. There were hundreds of rabbits on the plains. This may sound barbaric now, but at the time it was our only source of food. A group would clean the rabbits and prepare mushrooms for cooking while others cooked enough for several days. The military food arrived several days later. It never was as good as our rabbit feasts.

At last the TRR received its authorized number of brand new four-crew, twenty-eight ton, Matilda Infantry Tanks Mark II. What a beautiful sight. Unfortunately, not only were they too light but their one tiny two-pounder and Light Besa machine gun was no match for the German tanks armed with 88MM's. It was quite an event to train in these tanks on Salisbury Plains. The interior of the turret left just enough space for the tank commander, gunner and radio operator-gunner; none for claustrophobia. The driver was located near the front of the tank and had a hatch for entry and exit. The rest of the crew used the turret hatch. We were constantly warned about the possibility of losing fingers or finger tips if the turret hatch accidentally fell shut. Several fellows lost one or more fingertips at the first joint. Pappy Warmington was one of them. Unfortunately, after just six weeks training, our tanks were shipped to Russia to help them stem the Nazi tide sweeping into their country. Thus far, Operation Barbarossa had been a huge German military success.

On 25 July our Unit strength was 41 officers and 573 non-commissioned officers and enlisted men. On this date Canadian Corps Commander Lt. General McNaughton and British General Sir John Dill, Chief of Imperial General Staff inspected us.

One of the large tents housed the NAAFI (Navy, Army, and Air Force Institute), which was similar to an American Army Base Exchange except it didn't have as much merchandise. The troops shopped there for personal items and have a cup of tea with pastries when available. The NAAFI provided a good service for us since we lived under very austere conditions.

Sept 1, 1941

Dear Mother,

I'm fine and trust you all are well. As usual I've been very busy. More than ever. I haven't heard from you in quite some time and am wondering why. You never did acknowledge my first air-mail letter to you that was posted from Glasgow. I gave you my address for overseas but never received a letter addressed to me direct from home to here. August 12. I received a letter from you dated July 11. Also, haven't received parcel you mentioned as yet. You see by boat it takes about a month or longer for me to get a letter especially when they are addressed to Camp Borden and have to be redirected over here. I asked you to try and send them by air-mail via clipper ship which is much safer and I would get your letters in less than half the time.

By the way, one of your letters that was redirected to me from Camp Borden you asked me if I liked staying in London. Well the only time I was in London was on my debarkation leave which was for a 3 day leave there. I'm stationed "somewhere in England" but can't say where. Although not around London. We're out in the country. We just had a 40 day rain. Only a couple of days it didn't rain. I've never seen such a place for rain. Almost continuously.

As I said before we have no weekend passes. We get a 7 day leave every 3 months. I think my next leave will be in October. Haven't you seen any pictures of the Canadian Tank Corp or read any bit of news about it. I've seen quite a few of the Canadian papers with pictures and write-ups. I couldn't understand you saying that you heard that we were doing reconstruction work or something like that and known as "Red Caps". "Red Caps" are Lymie M.P.'s. We are working hard and doing intensive training.

The English country is very beautiful. The Shepherd with his sheep herding them over the downs. The farmer in his field and the old, old house in which he lives with thatched roof and the winding narrow lanes shaded with trees on both sides. Small villages like that of generations ago with inns and taverns like you see in the pictures of England in the time of Lord Nelson. The houses vine covered with flowers popping through here and there and their gardens fresh with variety of vegetables which supplies the farmers table. The uncommon sights of bicycles, some built for two. Small trains and automobiles. The Nobleman and the Gentry. It's all very interesting to me. Its lovely over here for a visit but I wouldn't live in this country still in the last century for anything. Our Sunday Church parade sometimes takes us to some old, very historic cathedrals. Not long ago we had the privilege of attending the services at the historic Salisbury Cathedral, which was built in 1027. It was the high Church of England. The Bishop of Salisbury after the services gave us an interesting account of the cathedrals history and the famous people, which were associated with it. I hope to go to London on my next leave. There are quite a few sights there I have yet to see.

One of my good friends, an American and in my troop, lost two fingers several weeks ago. The flap on the tank turret fell on his hand and chopped them off while he was inside and the tank moving.

As you know everything is rationed and we get very little tasty foods. It's difficult to even buy anything on leave especially candy, cakes, gum and its practically impossible to buy cigarettes. The only smokes we get are from home and those donated which are very few. You'll never realize what we're going through over here and smokes are very important to all of us as well as sweets and razor blades and other things which we have no way of getting and not able to buy. After all we're in the field and people on the other side should remember that we're the one's that are really doing the fighting and in constant danger and those little things to those at home mean everything to us. We all could use anything we could get. We pool everything we get as it is but to no avail. Also, it takes so long for anything to reach here from home. Its too bad that there is no one in the U. S. A. that could help the American boys over here with cigarettes and other things like the Canadians do by contributing to the Overseas Tobacco Leagues. Most of our fellows get 1,000 or 2,000 at a time but they don't last long. Other from what I mentioned above we all don't mind roughing it out at all which believe me we are doing.

I certainly would like to hear from you as often as possible because I'm always glad to receive your letters telling me how you all are getting along, etc. You will have to overlook my delays in writing to you all but they can't be helped. I would like for you to tell my friends to write to me because I would enjoy their letters very much.

Especially, Thurman, Jean H., Billy, Winifred, Con, Betty, Liza and Joan and I certainly could use anything to wear such as a scarf, socks, sweater, gloves and a handkerchief. You even have to go thru a lot of red tape to buy one handkerchief.

I would like to hear all of the local gossip in your next letter. By the way since I've been over here $25.00 a month is taken from my pay and is being saved for me till after the war or in case I get killed you will receive it. Have you received war-savings certificates from Canada yet?

I must go now so my best wishes and regards to all and the best of everything to you, Pat and Ed. Give my love to Grandma, Uncle Pat and Aunt Lou, Lillian and anyone else I didn't mention. Hoping to hear from you soon—All my Love to you all.

Your son,

Jack

Once or twice a month we went by the truckload into a nearby town to attend a local dance or frequent a pub as soldiers are prone to do. One Saturday night a near riot broke out as several fights started between British and Canadian troops; fights over girls or the lack thereof. The British troops were stationed several miles on the other side of this small town in the opposite direction. After a while things became nasty. The Military Police from both sides finally interceded and restored order. However, our troops said some of the British troops warned us never to return or they would throw us out of town. That was the wrong thing to say causing real trouble to brew. Some of our troops organized members of our regiment to go back into the town and teach those: "Limeys" a lesson. We planned to make our move the next Saturday. We told the British we would be there and to stay out of town! Our officers heard about our plan and immediately restricted everyone from leaving tent city and going into town. Would you believe some of our guys were so determined to go to town and finish the job that an all out effort was made to steal our own trucks and join the fight. They did just that! But when they got to town, not a British soldier could be found. They too, had been restricted to their base but they obeyed their officers. Maybe we forgot who the real enemy was. Well, all hell broke out within the TRR after this incident. Everyone who could be identified as a participant in the "Great Raid" was punished. Further, all TRR personnel were permanently restricted from ever going into town again. Fortunately soon afterwards, in September, the TRR was transferred to a new location.

We moved near a small village in Southern England. Early one morning we were awakened by a siren sounding the first air raid alarm since our arrival from Canada but no enemy aircraft were seen. Each tank squadron was located a few miles apart. We moved into a large manor house. This was a great improvement over "tent city". We were housed indoors and had a few other luxuries such as a kitchen, running water and bathrooms. It was difficult training without tanks for such a long time. We repeatedly performed the same monotonous tasks we were previously trained to do. For example, we went to Supply in the morning and checked out 7.92mm Bren machine guns. We took them to another building where we stripped, cleaned, oiled, reassembled them, put them back in their wood cases and returned them to Supply. Then we'd have lunch. After lunch we returned to Supply, checked out the same guns, and repeated the process all over again.

After what seemed forever the TRR received its assigned complement of five man, 38 ton Churchill tanks.

This was one big tank! It had a large Vauxhall, horizontally opposed engine with a huge gearbox. The extra man was a co-driver/gunner and sat next to the driver. It was equipped with two BESA machine guns and one two-pounder gun, which was later, replaced with a six-pounder (75mm) gun, which looked like a big cannon to me! The shells were about a foot long and were stored all around the inside of the big turret. Each crew had to take care of its tank, just like the old cavalryman had to take care of his horse. We didn't eat, clean up or do anything else until the tank was completely serviced and cleaned. This could take one to two hours or longer. We filled the one hundred seventy-five-gallon capacity fuel tank from "jerry cans" which held four gallons each, greased all the track wheels, topped off the oil, tightened the tracks then cleaned the whole vehicle. This could sometimes run into the night. Soon I felt I could do all the work blindfolded. Since the war, and now over fifty years later, the only thing I do with my car is put gas in it and take it to the dealer for periodic maintenance. Somehow I have no desire to see under its hood, let alone do any maintenance on it. My wife still doesn't believe I know a lot about engines.

11. DARK NIGHTS—DEATH—PEARL HARBOR

Our Brigade was assigned to guard the South Coast of England. Further, we continued to train with the First, Second, and Third Canadian Infantry Divisions. Since the TRR was located on the coast, German commandos would occasionally come ashore at night and capture or kill allied troops. For that reason I didn't like to perform guard duty at night. Periodically, I was assigned nighttime guard duty around the tank park. I patrolled an area that covered several hundred feet in each direction. Keep in mind there was a blackout. No lights anywhere. Combine this with a sometime dark, moonless night and it became a rather nerve-wracking duty. I wore a fully loaded .38 pistol at my side, and carried a Thompson sub-machine gun with a 50-bullet drum. My hand usually had a firm grasp on the gun handle, ready to fire by only releasing the safety. Often I had my back against a tree or post so I couldn't be attacked from the rear. When it's 2:00 a.m. and so black you can hardly see your hand in front of you its frightening. My adrenaline would start to rush when the wind blew and I heard the rustle of leaves. Was it a person sneaking up on me or just an animal foraging nearby? Often your eyes played tricks on you. Especially on a bright moonlit night when you sometimes thought you saw things but really weren't sure. We were told, as training procedure, British Commandos might surprise us in the dark to check our alertness. I'm glad that didn't happen to me because someone might have been shot. Actually, I did fire a few rounds at things during those long murky nights. Luckily, they were imaginary things and no one was hurt.

Periodically TRR provided a truck to transport us to nearby towns for recreation. One Friday night I went to a dance in a town over twenty miles away. The truck left promptly at 11:00 p.m. for the return trip. I was telling a young lady goodnight and barely missed the departing truck. I sure didn't want to be absent without leave (AWOL) so I had no choice but to walk back to my base. It was a beautiful moonlit night and I really didn't mind the 20-mile walk because the girl was worth every step of the way. I started walking at a very brisk pace but eventually slowed down a bit. I don't recall seeing a vehicle traveling in either direction. It took me about six hours to reach our base and my feet were in bad shape. I walked into the orderly room to check in from my evening pass. What a sight awaited me!

I was stunned! As I walked into the room one of our troopers was pointing a .38 revolver at our Sergeant Major, Pappy Powell. He told Pappy he was going to kill him. He saw me and told me not to move. I was petrified. I froze. As Pappy talked to the trooper, the NCO on duty, Sergeant Richardson, gradually inched his way closer to Trooper X. The trooper acted very strange and continued to threaten Pappy. I didn't move an inch, as Richardson kept getting closer. All of a sudden Richardson, a big man, jumped the trooper who was of slight build. He put a bear hug on him as both fell to the floor. Fortunately, the loaded pistol did not fire. Both Pappy and I helped restrain Trooper X who was escorted to an adjacent room. We put him on a cot where the NCO on duty usually slept during the night.

Pappy assigned Sergeant Richardson and me to guard Trooper X until the medics came. Trooper X was calm for a while, and then suddenly he would go berserk. He was like a wild man, sometimes frothing at the mouth. This guy really went off the deep end. Richardson was holding the top of Trooper X's body as I held his legs. He'd be very calm and lucid then without warning would become violent. We asked for help because it took all of our strength to hold him down. Soon, two more troopers joined us and we were able to keep him down during his violent periods. After a few hours the medics arrived. Trooper X was fairly calm as the doctor gave him a shot to keep him that way. A few minutes passed and the doctor told him to walk with him to the ambulance. I suggested to the doctor that the two medical technicians escort the patient but the doctor said Trooper X should be all right. About halfway through the building the patient grabbed the medical officer around the neck. Trooper X looked ferocious. I thought he would injure or kill the doctor before we could rescue him. Fortunately, the injection had started to take effect and a few of us were able to pull "X" off the Captain whose face was redder from embarrassment than injury. The trooper left in the ambulance secured and guarded by the medics. I never saw him again. I was totally exhausted. If only I had not missed the truck home!

The TRR went to the Gunnery Range at Minehead, Somerset (British Army) for a week of training; firing live rounds at various targets. This was our first experience shooting our two-pounders at mock-up tanks simulating battlefield conditions. Lucky for us no one fired back. We soon learned we had a long way to go to become proficient in gunnery and maneuvering our tanks. As a tank radio operator, one of my jobs was loading shells into the two-pounder. When fired there was quite a fast recoil and you had to make sure your hands were clear. The inside of the turret was cramped. We gave loading and firing commands with hand signals as well as radio intercom. The two-pounder, high explosive, armor piercing, tracer and other shells were stored around the inside of the turret. After firing a few rounds it was very hot, smelly and smoky inside the tank. As it turned out this practice was the closest I ever came to firing tank weapons in combat.

In mid-1941, I received a V-mail letter from my stepmother. It was bad news. Sad news. My father had died of a heart attack in Miami, Florida. He was only 56 years old. I was devastated. I went out to the nearby woods and cried my heart out. We had corresponded periodically and his letters were usually upbeat although apparently he was barely scraping by financially. There was no indication of any physical problems other than the usual colds from time to time. I felt very lonely and so very far away. I had virtually no one to turn to in this time of sadness. Even though I believed in God, I did not have a personal relationship with Him. However, I did pray to Him in times of dire need and I'm sure God knew my heart! This was one of those times.

---

7 December 1941—Japan attacks Pearl Harbor, Hawaii. U.S. Declares war on the Axis Powers (Japan, German and Italy)

Somewhere in England
Feb 10, 1942

Dear Mother,

I have received only 2 letters from you since before Christmas and no parcels. About a week before Christmas I received your parcel containing the scarf, etc. And wrote you a letter thanking you for the parcel. I'm sure that some of our mail must have been lost. Also, the mail truck caught on fire several weeks ago and 14 bags of mail were lost.

I received your last letter day before yesterday and a letter from Jean yesterday. I hope you all are well and doing okay. I have gained a few pounds and weigh between 150 and 155 lbs. and am feeling fine. Although I still have the same cold which is now a part of me. I hope the new year will bring to you all the best of everything and that we may be victorious this year. I wish I could have been with you all during the Holidays. I was well entertained in London by an American lady who has been in this country 6 years. She had the Eagle Club send 4 Americans out to her home for Christmas dinner. We all had a lovely time—turkey and all the trimmings, Christmas pudding and Champagne. The Eagle Club was certainly swell to all the fellows during the Holidays..dinners, dances, shows, parties, etc. were given for the boys and free tickets for shows. I went to the premiere of "A Yank in The R.A.F." and was given a 10s6d ($2.50) seat, which was contributed by Americans living over here.

Guess who I met here at a dance? Remember Harry Cookston? He's a friend of Thurman's and I used to go around with him occasionally. He only lives several blocks from us. He is in the U. S. Marines guarding the Embassy. It sure was swell seeing him and also another Chattanooga boy by the name of Ray Faeber in the C.T.T. He used to carry papers for the Times and knows Mr. Kiger. He lives in Red Bank. We had a nice time together. I met a ferry bomber pilot who knows Joe Wolf (ferry pilot) from Chattanooga. I met an U.S. Army officer (Lt.) from home but his name has slipped my mind. Anyway he is from Brainerd. It certainly is a small world isn't it? I'm sorry I couldn't have done something for you and Pat and Dad at Christmas but I just didn't have the money. As you know I only get half pay over here and breaking a pound note ($5.00 approx) is like busting a dollar bill at home. Everything is sky high. We have to save money for about 3 months to go on a 7 day leave and enjoy it. It takes between 10 and 15 pounds to sufficiently carry one through. I can well imagine how things are back home. Well it's 10 times worse here but we are used to rationing, high prices, etc. I was in London a short time ago and had an enjoyable time. I saw "Sgt. York" and it was a marvelous picture. Also "Sun Valley Serenade" from which the song "Chattanooga Choo-Choo" comes. I think it's a cute number. I've also seen "Blood and Sand", "The Sea Wolf", "Sullivan's Travels" and Bahama Passage" and they were all good pictures.

I've been to the American Embassy every chance I've had since the states officially came into the war, to see about transferring into the American forces the same as most Americans are doing and hope to do soon. The Embassy is awaiting word from Washington what to do with the Americans over here in the British Forces. I certainly do hope something happens soon because I'm really fed up just waiting. I should be in the U. S. Forces fighting for my own country instead of just marking time over here. I shall do my utmost to transfer.

I know you enjoy your Boy Scout work and Pat will he happy when he becomes a "Tenderfoot". Pat sure is taking up sports which is the thing he should do. What does he like best? I bet its football. How tall is he and how much does he weigh?

I'm sorry not to have answered Billy's. Con's. Mr. Redford's. Winifred's and other letters but I just don't have the opportunity. I enjoyed their letters very much and will you please thank them all for me. I would like to hear from them again soon. I don't know yet but I think I'll have to cut down on the writing I've been doing. I must go to dinner now so write to me real soon. My love to you all.

Your son.

Jack

P.S. Mother if it's straining your pocket-book to send the parcels..don't send them. I can understand that there's been quite a change in the economic situation and you will need all you have to get along on. But please don't stop the cigarettes and an occasional chocolate bar.

12. ON THE MOVE AGAIN

Early in 1942 the TRR moved to Worthing, a town near Brighton, the famous seaside resort on the English Channel. We were quartered in private homes in a section of town where many homes had been vacated. Due to the war, some owners were relocated elsewhere. This was a great improvement over our previous quarters. Each room housed several men sleeping on the floor on small, straw-stuffed mattresses. We had pillows and army blankets but the indoor plumbing was the highlight. The local people were appreciative and kind to us. We got used to the wailing sirens announcing the arrival of the Luftwaffe. German planes flew over Worthing regularly on their way to various targets. Often, on other occasions, several planes would bomb or fire their guns at random in the Worthing area wreaking havoc.

Monday, March 2, 1942

Dear Mother,

I received your Valentine and Birthday cards. Also the parcels including the flashlight, candy, etc.—and a package from R. J. Reynolds, all of which I'm very grateful to you. They certainly are a treat. For some reason I've only received about half a dozen letters from you since Christmas. I guess a lot of shipping has been lost. I know of several instances when we were informed that between certain dates that Jerry (Germans) had sent our mail to Davy Jones' locker (bottom of the sea). The last letter I wrote to you was about 2 weeks ago. The best way to keep track of our correspondence is to number your letters. Upon receipt of this

73

letter, which is No. 1 for me, you answer with letter No. 1 and so on. So if either of us get a letter that for example is No 6 and the last one received was No. 4, well we know then that No. 5 was lost.

I've been fine except for my cold, which is now a part of me. I hope you all are in the best of health.

I wish Pat a very happy birthday and many more to come. I would like to send a present to him but that is out of the question. It's very difficult to buy anything and when you do you are not allowed to send it out of the country. Also, you have to have (ration) coupons for nearly everything, which we don't have except for soap. (Soap is awfully scarce—I could use a couple of bars.) I'll try to get him a birthday card, which I may not be able to get because of the shortage of paper. All waste paper is salvaged and made into shells, ammunition, etc. Some places sell cigarette tobacco loose because of no paper.

So you see everything over here is save, save and save. I'm enclosing a newspaper clipping which states "its an offence to waste paper, burn or destroy paper or cardboard, throw it away; put it in a refuse bin or mix it with refuse. The penalty is 3 months in jail or 100 Pound ($500.00) fine, or both".

I got my monthly ration of one egg, which I enjoyed very much this morning. Mother, if you thought I ate a lot when

I was home, boy wait till I get back. I'll eat you out of house and home after eating our rations here. Especially your good cooking.

I received a very interesting 8-page letter from Jean. She is sending me a parcel, which is very sweet of her. I think quite a bit of Jean.

I guess you all are getting a taste of wartime conditions now. I can't tell you about over here the way things are concerning rations, clothing, etc. But I will have a lot to tell you when I get back. I guess by reading between the lines you get some idea of the way that things are.

I'm quite pleased with our new Camp. Although you wouldn't call it a camp because we are billeted in homes. Lovely brick houses in the residential district of a nice attractive city. We have civilian neighbors next door and then our fellows in the next house, etc. We live in houses of those who evacuated. It's a shame the way that some of the fellows damage the walls and floors. I guess though the owners will receive compensation from the government after the war.

This is the first city or town we've been stationed in. We have a good dance band in our Regiment and have a dance every Saturday night. We have quite a large crowd. We hold the dance in our Armory. Also, boxing matches, pictures, stage shows, bingo and other games. Its time we got some kind of a break.

It's strange to see vegetables growing over here in the winter. The People over here certainly are provident.

Do you ever see pictures of us in newsreels? Do you have blackouts yet or test air raid warnings? I hope that Pat had a very happy birthday. He'll be as big as me when I get back. I weigh around 160 lbs. now. There's one thing I would like you to send me. Or rather two things that are impossible to get over here. I've been meaning to ask you all along but forgot to. That is Mennen's After Shave Lotion and some hair oil. That's about all for now so close hoping to hear from you very soon.

Lots of Love to you, Pat and Dad

Your son,

Jack

Every Sunday all troops were required to attend either Catholic, Protestant or Jewish services. Each man joined a formation representing his faith. Since church services were mandatory the obligatory roll call was done. After several weeks I noticed the Jewish formation getting larger. Interestingly enough, the roll call went something like this: Dillon, Greenberg, O'Reilly, Horowitz, Shannon, Goldberg, O'Malley and so forth. The profusion of non-Jewish names was attributed to the Jewish Chaplain, or more precisely, his practice of giving each man a pack of cigarettes, a candy bar or a piece of fruit each week. News traveled quickly in our world. It didn't take long for some to discover what was considered the best deal on Sunday morning. The rest of us were marched to the local Anglican or Catholic Church for the morning service.

The U. S. entered the war on 7 December 1941. In the spring of 1942 newspapers informed us that Americans serving with Allied Military Forces could transfer to the U. S. Armed Forces. With a three day pass in hand I was off to London and the American Embassy to inquire how a transfer could be accomplished. The instructions were to submit the paperwork through my unit to the U. S. Officials. Immediately upon return to the TRR I asked to be transferred to the U. S. Army. Because of their investment in us, the Canadians seemed reluctant to release any Americans. Nevertheless, I assumed the transfer request would be processed. More on this later.

Periodically, we went into the beautiful English countryside on week-long maneuvers. Because of the war and possibility of a German invasion, there were no road signs. We had to depend on our maps to get from place to place. Fortunately, all troopers were proficient in map reading including the land gradient to insure our tanks could successfully traverse it. Few automobiles were on the road due to gas rationing.

Many things come to mind when I recall my first time away on maneuvers. Food has always been important to me and I recall vividly our 'gourmet' meals. Each five-man crew was issued ONE box of Iron Rations for each meal our food service crew did not prepare. It was a small box containing a can of corned beef, small tin of tea, sugar and jelly. There was also a tin of hardtack, which were two-inch, round crackers so hard they would almost break a tooth when you bit into them. For five grown or still growing men, this was about equivalent to a starvation diet. I was glad we weren't issued this delight very often. There were times when we came up with original ideas to expand our menu such as helping ourselves to a chicken from a nearby barnyard. While on maneuvers we received a welcome bonus if cooks were available to prepare breakfast. It came in the form of the standard British Rum Ration given each man. Going through the chow line the first thing we received was two jiggers of good Jamaican rum. Believe me, on an empty stomach this would warm the cockles of anyone's heart, especially on a bone-chilling English day. Some guys would trade a pack or two of cigarettes or something else for the teetotaler's rum ration.

As dusk approached our tank crew looked for a dry place to spend the night so we could escape the frequent rains of 'Jolly Ole England'. Crews sometimes slept under their tanks to keep as dry as possible. This rain deterrent ended when we learned a British crew did this and met their death. Their tank sank into the wet ground crushing them beneath it. One evening before dark we found an old dilapidated barn; it seemed an ideal place to spend the night with lots of hay to offer comfort for sleeping. Later, we went inside; each of us staked out our spot on the hay and quickly fell asleep. Sometime during the night we were awakened by strange sounds. We turned on our flashlights to find ourselves surrounded by huge, cat-sized rats. You never saw five guys move so fast! As we scattered, so did the rats. Needless to say, none of us got much sleep the rest of the night. I can remember that horrible experience just as though it happened yesterday.

The following afternoon traveling on a country road one of our tank tracks broke. Not having the tools or parts to repair it, we radioed for assistance. We learned it would be several days before help would arrive. In the meantime the rest of our squadron tanks continued on their mission. In the distance was a large structure, which appeared to be a manor house. We went to see if the owners could supply us with water. Imagine our surprise when a monk appeared at the door. We realized it was a monastery. When he heard our plight, we were welcomed like long lost brothers. The monks were most hospitable, providing food in addition to giving us the opportunity to enjoy their homemade bread, cheese, and wine. We had a marvelous time. We briefly thought about breaking the other track to extend our stay but quickly realized our duty lay elsewhere. Our brief time at the monastery and the hospitality shown us by the monks made up for those Iron Rations.

13. DOING IT THE HARD WAY—THE JAILBIRD

Back at the base I once again checked with the TRR Personnel Office to see if they had heard anything about my transfer to the U. S. Army. The answer was still "No"; I was getting anxious as several months had gone by since I first made inquiries. I decided to go to London to see the American authorities hoping they could help move things along. I got a weekend pass and learned the office I was to visit had moved. I would have to wait until Monday. At this point I had to make a difficult decision. Should I go AWOL until I could determine my status, or return to my unit? I opted to stay and find out once and for all if I could be transferred. It turned out I was shuffled from one office to another. Several days passed and I was getting antsy. Eventually I found the right office. I was told I was eligible for transfer but thus far the paperwork had not been received from the Canadian Army. With this news I was really in a quandary and didn't know what to do because officially I had been AWOL for some time.

I always tried to look spic and span in my uniform as I walked the streets of London. Once I asked a Canadian Military Policeman for directions hoping he wouldn't ask me for my long-expired weekend pass. Lucky for me he didn't. Finally I turned myself in to the Canadian Military Police. The next day a Canadian M.P. escorted me back to my unit. He was pleasant but I didn't like being handcuffed to him like a criminal. I was so embarrassed when people on the train looked at me and probably wondered what violent act that soldier had committed. When I arrived back at the TRR, I was put in the brig. I knew I was in deep trouble but had one thing in my favor. I had turned myself in to the military police and was not a deserter. I expected to be court martialed and at that time tell my story about my attempts to be transferred. I hoped my plea for help would fall on sympathetic ears.

A short time later, I was court martialed and sentenced to twenty-eight days at the Canadian Military Prison in Aldershot. This place was known as the "Glass House" because everything in it, including the people shined to perfection. What a miserable place. It was tent city all over again. Some of the men here were really bad characters. I was scared. I didn't know if the guys in my tent were murderers or what other terrible crimes they might have committed. I tried to have as little contact with them as possible. Most of the time we were kept busy working at various hard jobs. On top of the backbreaking work, it was very cold. Most of the time it was difficult to stay warm. We were never allowed to walk at a normal pace. Every place we went, including going through the chow line, we were required to move 'on the double', like a slow jog.

This was one of the lowest points in my life. What had gone wrong? I always wanted to do the right thing. I tried hard. I was a good soldier and eager to get into combat but nothing seemed to be going right for me. I wondered if the future had anything worthwhile in store for me. Where would I go from here? What would happen when I returned to my unit? What would my comrades think of me? Would I have any friends? I was really down in the dumps but fortunately I knew my mother and others were praying for me. At last, one of my worst experiences was over and I returned to the TRR. My commanding officer, Lt. Col. Jake Vining, had a fatherly talk with me and treated me kindly.

Shortly thereafter I was transferred with an honorable discharge to the American Army. It was on 3 September 1942, almost two years to the day I first enlisted in the Canadian Army. I was taken to a Quonset hut in a nearby town where the Canadians occupied one-half of the building and the Americans the other half. I went in the Canadian side a Canadian soldier and came out the other side an American GI. If you were a warm body and could walk, even with flat feet, and make it from one end of the building to the other, you were fit for service in Uncle Sam's Army. Nevertheless, I was elated that I passed both medical examinations. I went from $50.00 per month plus about $20.00 for trades pay (radio operator) with the Canadian Army to $30.00 per month in the United States Army. I certainly hadn't joined up for the money!

Finally I was in the American Army. Happy days! But wait! Happy days became somewhat tarnished because I had applied for an Army Air Force combat outfit but was assigned to the 32nd Military Police Company. About fifty men, all of who had transferred to the U. S. Army that day were "shanghaied" into the Military Police. Most of us were very upset to put it mildly.

14. A NEW START

What a difference a day makes! Yesterday I was in the Canadian Army and today in the U. S. Army! In comparing the two services I realized there were many positive things I gained from my training and experience in the Three Rivers Regiment. Fortunately, many have lasted a lifetime and proved beneficial to me. I benefited from the discipline that made me a self-starter and built into me the perseverance and determination to do the best possible job within my capacity and ability. I learned as they say to look adversity in the face and realize in due course of time I could overcome it and move on to better things. A positive attitude gave me the ability to turn lemons into lemonade. I learned and profited from mistakes I made in my early years as a green, and sometimes impulsive, young man. There were friendships that I remember to this day. I was at a very young, impressionable age and the two years I spent in the Canadian Army were a time of maturing for me. In retrospect it was very intense but I'll always be grateful to have had that experience.

The American Eagle Club
Sept 4, 1942

Dear Mother,

Sorry to have not written sooner but the past few months I have been busier than Churchill has. I've been to Wales and 6 different places in England in reference to my transfer.

Today I was sworn in to the U.S. Army and am now stationed in London. It took 9 months to get the transfer but it was worth waiting for. I'll probably get my uniform tomorrow. I'm really thrilled about the whole thing.

I hope you all have been enjoying the best of life. By the way, I just missed the Dieppe Raid. Our sister Regiment went over (The Calgary Tank) instead of us. They experienced heavy casualties. Be sure to write soon and my love to all. Don't send any parcels at all except cigarettes. The U.S. Army really feeds swell.

My address for the time being is:

Pvt. Jack Hubbard

10600328 U.S. Army, c/o American Eagle Club, London W.C.2, England,

Lots of Love,

Your Son,

Jack

The 32nd Military Police Company was located at 101 Piccadilly in the heart of the posh Mayfair district in the West End of London. We were about three short blocks from Hyde Park Corner and in the opposite direction about seven blocks to Piccadilly Circus, the Times Square of London. Our building was one of many in a row, adjoining each other but with individual architecture and design. The beautiful interior with marble floors, steps and staircases and huge lobby gave evidence to the fact this magnificent building must have previously served as a "Gentleman's Club". Most of the buildings were about five to seven stories high and the exclusive "Atheneum Club" was a few doors from us.

We used three floors and the basement. The rest of the floors were sealed off. The main floor included our dining room, kitchen and administrative offices. A small Army Base Exchange and supply office was located in the basement. One of our sergeants used to fill a duffel bag with cartons of cigarettes and sell them on the illegal "black market". He made a tidy sum of money before our Exchange was closed and a central one opened on Audley Street to serve the growing number of American troops in the London area. The new Exchange put Sarge out of business because they used ration cards. The other two floors were living quarters. We lived quite well with only one or two men assigned to a room. From our dining room windows we could look across Green Park and see Buckingham Palace.

I couldn't believe the food we were served. Every meal was a feast compared to the TRR. I never understood the vast difference in quantity and quality between the two services. We had an abundance of food at each meal. A typical lunch might consist of salad, roast loin of pork, potatoes, several vegetables, bread and dessert. I really did "pig out" during my first few weeks. To my surprise, there was a world of difference between the discipline in the Canadian and U. S. Army. The American Army was very lax compared to the TRR. This looked like it was going to be "tough duty". A piece of cake, so I thought.

The eastern side of our building bordered Whitehorse Street; a very narrow street running several hundred feet from Piccadilly to an area behind our building called "Shepherd Mews". Many people visited the mews. It was noted for its Bohemian lifestyle with artists, actors, high-priced call girls, restaurants, pubs, shops, apartments, Shepherds' market and other points of interest. We kept and maintained our vehicles, mainly Jeeps, in our garage, which opened on to Shepherd Mews. Several of our drivers became the paramours of some of the nearby girls of the night.

The 32ⁿᵈ Military Police Company was part of the 32ⁿᵈ Infantry Division, a National Guard unit from Michigan and, I believe Wisconsin and Illinois. After Pearl Harbor they were called to active duty and assigned to Camp Polk, Louisiana, for training. Race riots later erupted. Many soldiers were killed and injured. Since the 32ⁿᵈ M.P. Co. was directly involved, they were transferred to England. Possibly to avoid a Congressional investigation. This was common knowledge among our troops. I learned about it after joining the unit. In early 1942 there were few American troops in England.

WESTERN UNION Telegram, New York, N.Y. Nov 21, 1942

Mrs. O'Rear (my mother) =

WE ARE GLAD TO INFORM YOU THAT SPECIAL MESSAGE FROM YOUR SON BEING BROADCAST IN AMERICAN EAGLE CLUB PROGRAM NOVEMBER 21ˢᵀ 7:15 PM EASTERN STANDARD TIME OVER BBC SHORTWAVES 9.58 AND 11.75 AND 6.11 MEGACYCLES WE SHOULD BE GLAD TO HEAR HOW WELL YOU RECEIVE THIS PROGRAM= BRITISH BROADCASTING CORP 620 FIFTH AVE. NY.

15. WORKERS IN THE CASTE SYSTEM

The 32nd Military Police (MP) Company had about two hundred men in several platoons. Our commanding officer was Captain James P. Mullane. There were several second lieutenants. I soon learned this unit epitomized the caste system at its worse. There were four castes from top to bottom. At the top were several regular Army non-commissioned officers including the first sergeant (who was given a direct commission as a first lieutenant a few months later). Next were the "home town boys" from the National Guard, representing the bulk of the troops. The draftees, who got little respect from the National Guard soldiers, followed them. At the bottom were us lowly transferees from the Canadian Army who usually got the short end of the stick.

After a couple of months it didn't take long to figure out who got most, if not all, of the promotions awarded; the "home town boys" of course. I knew there wasn't any future for me in this outfit. I wanted to see action. I wrote a letter to my commanding officer requesting I be transferred to the U. S. Army Air Force, which were the only American forces engaged in combat at the time. I still have a copy of that letter. I was told I could not be transferred. Every month I submitted my letter requesting a transfer. Each month my Commanding Officer said "No". I don't believe my letter was ever submitted to the next higher level in the chain of command for their approval or disapproval. Three of my buddies who had transferred from the Canadian Army had also started their monthly letter campaign requesting transfer to an appropriate combat unit whereby their previous training in the Canadian Army could be best used. Their requests reached the same dead end as mine. Their morale was very low; so was mine.

We had four platoons; each one assigned specific duty, which was usually rotated on a weekly basis. One platoon did daytime foot patrol around the Piccadilly Circus area, while another patrolled it at night. A third guarded U. S. installations and properties while the fourth trained. When we first started patrolling the Piccadilly Circus area we used only six pairs of MPs. There was a dramatic buildup of American forces during the sixteen months prior to January 1944, which was the period I served with the 32nd M.P. Company. I believe there were over two million American soldiers in England prior to the invasion of Europe on D-Day 6 June 1944. Some voiced fear the island might sink because of the huge number of American troops stationed there.

By September 1943 we had increased our foot patrol around Piccadilly Circus to about twenty-five pairs of MPs! Remember, at night, it was blackout; our job was to keep the GIs moving along. There were over two thousand prostitutes within one mile of Piccadilly Circus and they were propositioning every GI they saw until they scored. GIs who drank too much became a serious problem. Those in bad shape were taken to a Red Cross Club and put to bed for the night. Their wallet was put in a safe place until they "slept it off". Another problem were the few prostitutes and thieves who "rolled" drunk GIs and took their money and anything else of value. We also checked for passes to make sure the soldiers had a valid pass or leave papers. Considering the number of men we dealt with, there were few fights.

Any time we had a serious problem with our troops we had no choice but to take them to the "pokey". When Army Air Force combat flight crews were taken to jail for rowdiness due to drunkenness they would sober up somewhat after a few hours and request permission to call their base. We were usually told to release them immediately because they were scheduled to fly a mission the next day. We released them. How about that! Overall, the majority of our troops were well behaved and caused no problems. One afternoon while patrolling

Piccadilly Circus I saw a dozen or so soldiers walking together. The man in front was an Army first sergeant. I checked his pass. He and the other men, all from the same outfit, had been AWOL for a week. Undoubtedly, disciplinary action was in order for these men when they were returned to their units. It crossed my mind that maybe this was a form of mass protest. Perhaps these men had similar problems like I experienced trying to get a transfer.

16. THE WAR WASN'T ALL BAD

There were plenty of young ladies available to meet at dances at the American Red Cross Clubs in London and other dance halls like the huge Covent Garden and Hammersmith Palais. Often, pubs were the social gathering places of the day. Different military units sponsored dances and gatherings as well. There was a shortage of English men since the British had been in the war since 1939. Many of their soldiers were overseas. There was an article in one of the London newspapers that stated, "American soldiers are overpaid, oversexed and over here". Some American replied saying "English soldiers were underpaid, under sexed and under Eisenhower."

One night I took a girl to Covent Garden. The main floor of the famous Opera House had been converted to a huge dance hall. Top orchestras played almost every night. We were sitting at a table in a dimly lit area. I reached over and tapped a guy on the back and asked him for a light for my cigarette. Matches were in short supply during the war. He turned around and I was surprised to see Harry Cookston, a friend of mine from Chattanooga. Harry was a Marine Lance Corporal guarding the American Embassy. We met several times afterwards and then he shipped out to an unknown destination. The next time I saw him was in Chattanooga in 1944. He was a sergeant and had served with the First Marine Division in the Pacific. He had earned two Purple Heart medals for wounds received during combat against the Japanese.

London's civilian population was about seven million people. There were also a large number of refugees from all over Europe who worked at a variety of jobs. The professional entertainers were the cream of the crop and gave outstanding performances in restaurants and nightclubs before packed houses. About a mile from my quarters were several blocks of housing set aside for European Jewish refugees. They were taken care of by the British government and had to abide by certain rules. One was an evening curfew. I remember this quite well because I had several dates with a beautiful Jewish girl whose last name was Bloom. While in New York City in 1951 I got on a subway train and to my amazement sat down in front of Ms. Bloom. She introduced me to her husband, a former GI she had met and married while in London. What a coincidence. They lived in New York but I was there only for a few days.

London had a staggering number of military personnel from all over the world. The British Empire was represented by some sixty countries plus many European countries including the French, Belgian, Dutch, Norwegian, Danish, Polish, Yugoslavians, Czechs, and others. There were probably over one hundred different uniforms represented by the Army, Navy and Air Forces of these countries. One afternoon the British Army had two of their people dressed in German Army officer's uniforms. They walked along the busiest part of Piccadilly for almost an hour before someone recognized the uniforms. Apparently, the Brits wanted to know how observant people were.

I was always fascinated to see the Indian Siks and Ghurkas in their unique uniforms with their heads wrapped in turbans. Some of these soldiers were fierce looking to say the least. They not only carried rifles but also had daggers in their belts. I heard that during World War I when the Ghurka's left their trenches and attacked the German lines they would cut off an ear of each German they killed and bring back as proof of their kill. It brings to mind the old "Wild West" when the gunslingers put a notch in their gun handle for each man they killed.

Poland had several fighter squadrons in the R.A.F. Their pilots were noted for their bravery in combat. I knew one of these pilots. He shot down a German plane and was chasing another one when his ammunition ran out. He didn't quit the engagement but flew into the German plane. As he crashed into it he bailed out and watched his and the German planes disintegrate in mid-air. He received one of Poland's highest decorations for this extraordinary act of bravery. The top brass probably weren't too happy about losing the aircraft.

My favorite watering hole was a popular place called Universal Brasserie, centrally located at Piccadilly Circus. I found this pleasant restaurant/pub while serving with the Canadian Army. I soon knew most of the key people who worked there. Harry Bolger, the cloakroom attendant, became a personal friend. Periodically, Harry would invite me to his home for dinner and I enjoyed being with him and his family. One thing for sure you could count on was lots of girls, usually twosomes, having a drink or dinner, at the Universal Brasserie. Some were in uniform and others were civilian working girls such as secretaries and clerks. It was a great place to meet girls. It was easy to get to because it had an entrance at the bottom of a flight of steps from Piccadilly Circus. Another entrance led into the restaurant from the Piccadilly Tube (Subway) station. Since food was scarce I really enjoyed the sautéed mushrooms that were sometimes on the menu. They were large, tastefully prepared and served with fresh French bread. Sometimes I would eat two orders. They were both delicious and nourishing. The restaurant had two bars, one for beer and the other for liquor. Sometimes my bartender friends would take a one-pound English note from me for a glass of beer and give me back change totaling one pound. Many servicemen got breaks like this because most people appreciated and fully supported military personnel.

The government closely regulated drinking establishments. Most bars opened at 11:00 a.m. and closed at 2:00 p.m. They reopened at 5:30 p.m. and closed at 10:30 p.m. for the night. A few minutes before closing time, one of the bartenders would yell out, "Time gentlemen, time!" This meant you had to hustle to get your last drink before closing. Sometimes it seemed like a stampede with everyone trying to get one more drink for the road. When the whiskey bar opened in the evening there was usually a queue several men deep waiting to order their first drink. Usually, there was a run on Scotch first. When that was gone, gin was next and so on through the different liquors. Sometimes there was enough to go around for everyone that night. The beer bar had several men working hard to keep up with the demand. R.A.F. (Royal Air Force) flyers, mainly fighter pilots as well as a few U.S. military always patronized this place. R.A.F. Fighter pilots were easily recognized because they did not button the top button on their uniform jacket. I often saw R.A.F. pilots who had been horribly burned before bailing out of their planes. This happened because the aircraft gas tanks were not sealed or there was no armor plate behind the pilot. Many were disfigured and were going through stages of surgery to replace missing parts on their faces.

These were the true heroes of the Battle of Britain. My heart went out to those brave men who made such a great sacrifice for their country. They were some of the men Prime Minister Winston Churchill spoke about during one of his speeches when he said, "Never in the field of human conflict was so much owed by so many to so few".

I learned about several illegal black market restaurants which served "steaks" with eggs and chips (French-fried potatoes) and a few other foods not available elsewhere. These restaurants were difficult to get into because a regular patron had to vouch for you initially. Afterwards, you could gain entrance with a password. It reminded me of the old speakeasies in the U. S. during prohibition.

It was a special treat for me to occasionally enjoy one of these pricey meals.

The steak in most cases was horsemeat. I couldn't tell much difference except it tasted a bit sweeter than beef. The steak was cooked to perfection with a couple of fresh fried eggs on top with plenty of chips. I patronized several small legitimate restaurants occasionally and eventually became friends with the owners. I befriended a couple of them, Henry and Harry. They greatly appreciated cigarettes and other scarce items I gave them. When stationed in the London area in 1951 I went to a large, beautiful restaurant in the West End. Much to my surprise the owner was Henry. We greeted each other like long lost brothers! My money was never any good in his restaurant so I didn't go there often because I did not want to take advantage of our friendship.

17. A LONDON AIR RAID

When the Germans approached London to drop their bombs the air raid sirens with their unmistakable wailing sound alerted people so everyone would have sufficient time to reach an air raid shelter. Several nights while on duty at Piccadilly Circus an attack was imminent. I helped an English Bobby (policeman) clear the streets of people as fast as possible into the Piccadilly Circus Underground (Subway) station which was used as an air raid shelter. The Bobby told me to avoid standing near glass windows or doors because nearby exploding bombs created flying glass shards which could cause serious injury or death. As we assisted people to the shelters I heard anti-aircraft guns firing away at the approaching bombers and the exploding bombs. All of this was a scary and chilling sound. But the frightful sound paled in comparison when seeing the ghastly and horrible scene just after bombing.

After the last people went into the shelter, we made a quick check of the area to make sure no one was still outside. Most of the time I went in to the shelter and waited until the "All Clear" siren sounded. Usually, it was over in twenty to forty minutes. The shelters were packed with people like sardines because many families, couples and singles slept there every night. This was the case in most underground stations. A couple of times I stayed outside in the blackout watching the action taking place in the night sky. Most of the time it was difficult to find a safe place which if hit by a bomb would protect me from flying glass. It was jokingly said if a bomb hit the nearby Regent Palace Hotel, most of the mighty Eighth Air Force flyers would be killed. Later a bomb hit the hotel and a few American flyers were killed and injured.

One night during an air raid some of us off-duty Military Policemen made our way to the top of our building and walked to several adjoining buildings. The ack-ack guns across the street in Green Park started firing away at German bombers. The noise was deafening. As guns fired a series of rounds in quick succession, they made a very loud noise that sounded like a rapid Boom, Boom, Boom, Boom, Boom. What a grandstand seat we had...seeing the searchlights scanning the skies for enemy planes, the sound of the bomber engines and anti-aircraft guns blasting away! Soon it happened. You've heard the old adage "everything that goes up must come down". It started raining shrapnel from the shells that were fired at the enemy planes. We couldn't move fast enough to reach a safe place. Fortunately, no one was hit. I should have known better because we were trained to direct people out of danger from falling objects during an air raid. I guess curiosity got the best of us but we learned our lesson in a hurry.

It was awful looking at the results of the bombings. Sometimes, the huge craters were half a block long creating one big mess. There was also tremendous damage from the fires. It was amazing to see the positive attitude of the people as they quickly cleaned up the debris after an air raid.

I have tremendous respect for the British people. They were courageous, determined and tenacious during the war. They alone bore the brunt of the vicious Nazi air attacks for over two years. At first the Germans attacked military targets. When that failed to get the anticipated results they bombed the civilian population hoping the British would surrender. As in past history when there is a dire need for outstanding leadership someone appears on the scene. In this case it was Prime Minister Winston Churchill who I believe was the greatest statesman and political leader in the twentieth century. His many great speeches were awesome and inspiring. After becoming Prime Minister he told the nation, "I have nothing to offer but blood, toil, tears and sweat."

Shortly thereafter on 4 June 1940 the German Army defeated the French and British Army in France. Ships and small personal pleasure boats from England miraculously evacuated British personnel along with a number of French military totaling 338,226 from Dunkirk, France on 4 June 1940. However the British Expeditionary Force lost over one thousand guns and all of its equipment.

When things looked the bleakest and truly hopeless Churchill rallied the British nation with his famous speech:

"Even though large tracts of Europe and many old and famous states have fallen or may fall into the grip of the Gestapo and all the odious apparatus of Nazi rule we shall not flag or fail. We shall go on to the end. We shall fight in France. We shall fight on the seas and oceans. We shall fight with growing confidence and growing strength in the air. We shall defend our island, whatever the cost may be. We shall fight on the landing grounds. We shall fight in the fields and in the streets. We shall fight in the hills. We shall never surrender."

18. FROM BAD TO WORSE—FRANCE FALLS

On 17 June the French sued for peace. This left Britain alone to fight the huge Nazi war machine and disaster appeared imminent. The feared German invasion of England could come at any moment. The next night Churchill spoke again giving the reasons for losing the battle in France. He pointed out the need for coming success in the air. "I do not at all underrate the severity of the ordeal which lies before us but I believe our countrymen will show themselves capable of standing up to it. Every man and woman will have the chance to show the finest qualities of their race and render the highest service to their cause. Our professional advisers of the three services advise that there are good and reasonable hopes of final victory. We have also consulted all the self-governing dominions and I have received from their Prime Ministers messages, couched in the most moving terms, in which they endorse our decision and declare themselves ready to share our fortunes and to persevere to the end.

The Battle of France is over. The Battle of Britain is about to begin. Upon it depends our way of life. The whole fury and weight of the enemy must very soon be turned on us. If we fail, the whole world will sink into an abyss of a new Dark Age, made more sinister, and perhaps more protracted, by the lights of perverted science. Let us therefore brace ourselves to our duties, and so bear ourselves that, if the British Empire and Commonwealth last for a thousand years, men will still say, "This was their finest hour."

The Germans believed they could defeat England by daily air attacks with hundreds of bombers followed by invasion. It was the Battle of Britain that turned the tide for England. There was always the threat of a German invasion of England during the first several years of the war. The British were woefully unprepared for this potential threat. Those who were not on active duty in the armed forces were usually assigned to the Home Guard, which consisted mainly of men too old or not medically qualified to serve. Most of them did not have uniforms. They drilled with hunting rifles, shotguns, broomsticks, pitchforks and the like. They never complained. Through it all, they maintained their wonderful sense of humor. Sometimes they shared their meager rations with someone less fortunate. When invited to their home for a meal I was almost too embarrassed to eat. I always took whatever I could to help them out. Usually candy bars, cigarettes, cookies, peanuts and other scarce goodies. I felt sorry for the youngsters. It was really rough on some of these little kids but they kept a stiff upper lip like their parents.

Most GIs had a soft place in their heart for these kids. We usually carried gum and candy for them. Quite often they asked, "Got any gum, chum?" All of these items were rationed along with others such as soap, razor blades, matches, juices, etc. Each soldier was issued an Army exchange Ration Card valid for two months. It was replaced upon expiration. These cards listed the rationed items with corresponding columns headed by each week of the two-month period. Each time a soldier bought an item the card would be stamped with a red dot indicating the week it was purchased. Ration cards had to be signed by the soldier and the issuing authority.

19. EXCITING LONDON AND THE 32ND M.P. COMPANY

Soon after my assignment to the 32nd M.P. Company in September 1942, I met a lovely young lady named Pat. She was a blue-eyed blonde with a heart that matched her beauty. Pat had an effervescent personality that always made me feel good and warm inside just to be with her. Her father worked for the Shepperton movie studio near Putney Bridge where they lived. Pat had a younger brother about fourteen years old who reminded me of my brother Pat. I visited in their home on several occasions. They were always gracious and hospitable to me. Pat's mother treated me like one of the family, which made me feel comfortable. Her father and I got along very well. One day he arranged a tour of the studios for me, which I found most enjoyable. It was interesting learning from an expert how movies were made. He worked there for many years and was highly respected in the industry.

Pat and I dated for several months and were becoming serious about each other. As we saw each other more frequently, I realized my initial infatuation with her was soon replaced with a growing, passionate love for her. I could hardly wait for our next date to see her. Each moment away from her was like an eternity. I called her one night but there was no answer. The line seemed dead. I called the next couple of days with the same result. I became worried and contacted a British government agency to find out why I couldn't get through to her. They checked their records and said a bomb had hit their home and all members of the family had been killed.

All members of the family had been killed. Those words haunted me. I couldn't believe it. I checked with the agency and the studio again to make sure someone had not been mistaken. They hadn't. It was a shocking loss. The war had now touched me personally and deeply. It took some time for me to realize I would never see Pat or her family again. As the war progressed and many more lives were lost I realized more and more how precious life really is.

Most people attended the movies often. It was a means of escape to get away from the war for a couple of hours. American pictures were very popular. I especially enjoyed them because in a sense it was a connection to home. I frequently went to movie theaters in Piccadilly Circus and Liecester Square, a 15-minute walk from my quarters on Piccadilly. Almost everyone was wild about the Glenn Miller Orchestra. I remember seeing him and his band in the movies "Sun Valley Serenade" and "Orchestra Wives". Before the war, I saw them in person in Louisville, Kentucky. One of the most popular British orchestras was "Geraldo and his Orchestra". He had the 'Miller Sound' and performed regularly on the British Broadcasting Corporation (BBC) radio stations.

At the conclusion of each movie, everyone in the theatre stood at attention as the flags for England, United States, France and the USSR were shown on the screen. The appropriate national anthem was played with English words shown on the screen and everyone was expected to sing. This took a fair amount of time to complete. In the event of a pending air raid a notice was flashed on the screen stating that all who wished to leave for the air raid shelters should do so at that time. Later, when the 'all clear' was sounded, a message to that effect was shown on the screen. Most people stayed in the theatre. Sometimes you could hear anti-aircraft guns firing away at German aircraft along with exploding bombs nearby. This wasn't exactly a morale booster!

Many popular songs were performed by British and American artists during the war. Some most often heard were "I'm Dreaming of a White Christmas" (Bing Crosby), "The White Cliffs of Dover" (Vera Lynn), "Paper Doll" (Mills Brothers), "All or Nothing at All" (Frank Sinatra), "Bugle Call Rag" (Andrews Sisters), songs by Nat 'King' Cole and others. People of all ages liked the popular music of the day. London dance halls were usually well attended both day and night. The larger ones, Covent Garden and Hammersmith Palais, usually rotated two bands each night. This was a great place to meet young ladies. It was proper to ask a girl to dance a set of music and then a different girl for the next set.

I met a lovely girl named Joyce. She was blonde, blue-eyed and about five feet three with a figure that would put Venus de Milo to shame. She was a pretty girl with a great sense of humor. There was something about her that reminded me of Pat. Maybe that was what I wanted to believe. Nevertheless she came along at the right time filling a void in my life. I saw her frequently because we enjoyed each other's company. We always seemed to have a good time together regardless of the wartime pain and suffering which continually surrounded us. I met her mother and father and younger brother. Occasionally, her parents invited me to their home for a meal sharing their meager rations; usually a minuscule piece of meat if available, potatoes and brussel sprouts. There seemed to be a never-ending supply of brussel sprouts since most everyone had a "Victory Garden." I always brought whatever food and goodies I could scrounge up, especially nuts, cigarettes, candy and gum. I got along fine with her family. It was a treat visiting with them because it was like being part of a family once again. I became misty eyed as I recalled the good times spent with my own family, which seemed like a millenium ago.

I was twenty-one years old and so much had already happened in my life. Fortunately, I usually remembered only the good things I had experienced, not the bad. Being with Joyce and her family was a special time for me. It was my impression that Joyce and I were becoming more serious about each other as time went by. You may wonder why the budding romance with Joyce after losing Pat. Every moment in those unpredictable days was very precious to me. Living in the midst of a war zone where people were being killed every day added the ingredient of urgency to my life, the urgency to savor every minute of life to the fullest. The feelings I had then are difficult to convey because without personally experiencing them, the key to their understanding is lost forever.

I had been a member of the 32nd M.P. Company about six months and stil submitted my monthly request for transfer to the Army Air Force. But my Company Commanding Officer gave his regular standard reply...No! During this period of time there had been a significant buildup of American military forces in England, particularly in London. We no longer guarded military facilities and our training had been greatly reduced since it was repetitive. Weather permitting we trained across the street in Green Park. Green Park had a series of trenches strategically placed to afford some form of protection during air raids. It was a large beautiful park with sidewalks winding through pretty trees and plants. Anti-aircraft guns, barrage balloons and searchlights were located in the park. Women staffed most of these military units.

One interesting aspect of our training included defending oneself with just our hands against any size assailant. Techniques were used whereby exerting pressure on opponents would make them suffer extreme pain easily bringing them to their knees. Also, there were certain ways for striking individuals with your hand that rendered them unconscious or with the right blow kill them. Obviously, these were last-ditch stands against a violent opponent.

Our walking patrol was beefed up due to the additional American troops in London. There were always at least two jeeps on patrol. One included the officer of the day, a driver, and one or two men. The other jeep had the non-commissioned officer of the day with the same complement of men.

London is a fabulous city, one of the great cities of the world. Because of my duties I quickly became familiar with London. There is so much to see with many interesting places to visit. It is steeped in tradition and history. Getting around was easy because London had the best transportation system in the world. Buses and underground trains ran every few minutes and hundreds of taxis were available charging reasonable fares.

As a young man I was fascinated with London, the capital of the British Empire. I could hardly believe I actually lived in this exciting city. Every place I went was not only interesting but also seemed to have significant historical value. Some of my favorite places were the River Thames, the Houses of Parliament, Big Ben in the Clock Tower, Westminster Abbey, Tate Gallery, Trafalgar Square, Changing the Guard at Buckingham Palace, the National Gallery, St. Paul's Cathedral, the Tower of London, the Tower Bridge, Hyde Park, Kensington Gardens, the British Museum, Regent's Park, the London Zoo and other places. Many were within walking distance from my quarters. I stopped often at St. Martins-in-the-Field Church at Trafalgar Square for a hot cup of tea. It really hit the spot, especially on those cold, bone-chilling winter nights London is noted for.

I always enjoyed going to the American Eagle Club at 28 Charing Cross Road to rest and relax. A lovely American lady, Mrs. Frances Dexter, with the help of a Brit, Mrs. Blake, started the club. Initially it was for the benefit of Americans who were serving in the R.A.F. Eagle Squadron, which was formed prior to the United States entering World War II. It was a place where American flyers could meet and enjoy a bit of Americana. Later the club accepted all Americans serving with allied military forces. The Eagle Squadron had an outstanding combat record during the Battle of Britain and afterwards. Many of these officers later transferred to the U. S. Army Air Force and continued making a significant contribution to the air war. "A Yank in the R.A.F," an American-made war movie, depicted some of the exploits of American volunteers flying in the RAF.

While serving in the TRR I always went to the American Eagle Club whenever I was on leave in London. It certainly filled emptiness in my life since there were no Red Cross Clubs available at the time. I enjoyed the fellowship with other Americans, which provided my closest connection with home.

I was assigned a new duty periodically which I looked forward to and enjoyed. It was the Embassy mail run to Scotland. Every night the U. S. Embassy mail, sealed in mail pouches, was picked up in London by two MPs. It was guarded en route and delivered to the authorities at Prestwick Airfield near Ayr, Scotland. The U. S. Air Transport Command C-54 aircraft flying between the U. S. and the British Isles used this major air base. Our train departed at night and arrived at Prestwick the next morning. We had our own compartment and literally guarded our highly classified material with our lives. Our loaded guns were handy and ready for use if necessary. In these war time circumstances it was easy to imagine the enemy boarding the train and blowing us away, taking highly classified sensitive documents vital to the war effort. We also had to consider the possibility of being attacked by the 'Fifth Column'. These were English traitors working for the enemy. Of course they were indistinguishable from ordinary folks. Could some of these people be on board? Believe me, we stayed on high alert and hopefully ready for any event.

On one trip in May 1943 we finished delivering the pouches to personnel aboard a waiting C-54 at Prestwick. As usual, we went to the terminal for a snack. While walking in the terminal we saw an unusual sight. There were two prisoner-of-war groups escorted by American and British officers. These were not the usual POWs. One group consisted of several Italian generals. The other were German generals headed by Colonel General Hans-Jurgen von Arnim (equivalent to U. S. 4-star general) all wearing their desert khaki uniforms. General von Arnim had replaced 'the Desert Fox' Field Marshal Erwin Rommel, as Commander of all Axis Forces in Africa. Von Arnim was captured on 12 May 1943 at his Afrika Korps headquarters in Tunisia, Africa. He was the second-highest ranking German prisoner in western hands (after Rudolf Hess) at the time of his capture. The German officers ignored the Italians and would have nothing to do with them. It was fascinating to watch all of this activity from a nearby vantage point...seeing history in the making.

About midway in the terminal the POWs were turned over to a group of high-ranking American and British officers who saluted General von Arnim, talked for a few minutes then everyone left the terminal. This scene was evidence of the Allies first big victory, the defeat of the German and Italian armed forces in North Africa. This was a huge morale booster after a prolonged period of bad news from all the allied war fronts. It was later rumored that General von Arnim stayed at the very posh Claridge's Hotel in London's West End at Churchill's request hoping he would divulge some of the Nazi's secrets which would benefit the Allies war effort.

July 1, 1943

Dear Mother,

I received your letters and very glad to hear from you. Sorry to hear that you are still feeling ill. I trust that you will recover completely.

Speaking of letters, I'm always glad to hear from you but I detest V-Mail. I would much rather wait a while longer and get a genuine letter which I appreciate so much more. Today is my second anniversary in England. Soon I shall have 3 years service. A short time back another M.P. and myself went to Scotland on Special Duty. This is the second trip on this duty and like the idea of getting away from the regular routine. I had a good game of golf while I was up there and certainly did enjoy it. While visiting the Red Cross Club there I met Kay Curtis from Chattanooga. I only chatted with her for a few minutes because I had to be on my way.

I'm still working on my transfer to the Air Corp and if everything goes okay I should be flying in several months from now.

The weather over here is beautiful. The scenery from Southern England to Scotland is absolutely gorgeous. We have been getting strawberries and cherries that are delicious. While in Scotland I saw 2 Italian generals and 3 German generals. The Germans wouldn't have anything to do with the Italians. The Italians looked hopeless but the Germans tried to put up a front and looked stern and arrogant but you could look in to their eyes and see that they were defeated and that the Germans had lost and that we are the victors and conquerors.

Bob Hope will be in person at a show on July 4th here and I know the place will be jammed by Americans and also the English who are very fond of him.

I can't understand why I haven't heard from Jean Hart. She must not have the correct address. I'm proud of Pat making so many 'As'. I sure would like to see him. I bet he's nearly as big as me now. Glad to know that he is taking up sports. He should be as active as possible. I try to get as much exercise as possible over here. I must say "so long" for now. Please give my best wishes to all. With all my love to you, Pat and Dad,

Your son,

Jack

Because of the large and rapid influx of troops in the London area arrangements were made whereby Scotland Yard would provide the 32nd M.P. Company two unmarked police cars to enhance our mutual cooperation and effectiveness. Guess what? The tedious Morse Code training with the TRR paid off! I was selected, along with three other MP's to attend four months of training at Scotland Yard. This was a privileged experience for us. Everyone at Scotland Yard was most helpful and extended us every courtesy. They gave us a tour of their infamous "Black Museum," which most people are not permitted to see. It was both fascinating and bizarre. It contained various implements and objects of crime, which had been confiscated from criminals, perverts and deviates.

It was incredible to see things that people used against other people. It defied one's imagination: man's inhumanity to man. I was impressed with Scotland Yard's operational efficiency, which directly reflected upon their personnel's knowledge and dedication to duty. I'm sure that's why they are so famous for tracking down criminals and bringing them to justice.

When our training was completed, Scotland Yard provided the 32nd M.P. Company with two large four-door sedans with a radio receiver in each trunk. The radio operator wore a headset but could only receive Morse code messages from the Scotland Yard radio transmitter. He also had a lighted clipboard with message forms to record messages. We did not have transmitters therefore were unable to acknowledge receipt of messages. Thus all messages to the patrol cars were sent twice.

Four men were assigned each car as previously described for the jeeps. What a difference between the jeeps and cars, especially in cold, windy and wet weather.

These cars were used to patrol areas frequented by GIs and to check on our foot patrols. Driving in London during the blackout could be tricky business. Only the left front headlight allowed a small sliver of light to shine onto the road, which meant constant defensive driving in the dark. During our nightly rounds we went to dance halls and monitored the behavior of American soldiers. While on duty, we wore a brassard on our left arm with the letters M.P. that identified us as Military Policemen.

As it turned out, this identification served a dual purpose, which enhanced our social life. It didn't take long for young ladies to figure out Military Policemen were stationed in London. It made it a little easier for us to meet some nice girls even though we were on duty. I suppose this could be considered a fringe benefit. As I've often heard, "even a blind pig finds an acorn once in a while."

American Red Cross Clubs were a godsend for our troops. The 'Rainbow Corner' Club was a five-story building located very close to Piccadilly Circus. American girls with a sprinkling of British staffed it. Being an MP,I knew most of the staff. Sally Elton from Massachusetts was in charge, I believe, with a real southern beauty named Miss Sippi as her assistant. We GI's called her Mississippi. Every effort was made to ensure that soldiers and sailors felt the closeness of home. Meals and snacks, hospitality, information and recreation were available twenty-four hours a day. Our military personnel on leave were provided lodging at several clubs for fifty cents a night, breakfast included. Troops were also provided directions and maps to various points of interest in London.

Dances were held almost every night of the week at the various clubs. The most popular was the Glenn Miller orchestra who performed periodically in the area. Another U. S. Military band, based in London, played regularly duplicating the Miller sound. I enjoyed their music so much I followed them from Red Cross Club to Red Cross Club whenever I could.

When flyers completed their tour of combat missions, Rainbow Corner made them members of their 'Happy Warriors Club'. Rainbow Corner celebrated its first anniversary on 5 December 1943. Five million U. S. Armed Forces members and their guest visited Rainbow Corner during its first year. I was fortunate to attend this wonderful celebration.

The following is quoted from the back of a handout, "Instructions For Men On Leave", issued by Special Service Office, HQ. LONDON BASE COMMAND:

"If your pass does not say, or you have not been told by your officer where you will stay, or if you are lost or need assistance, phone GERrard 5616 or ask your way to Rainbow Corner. London Bobbies and our military police are interested in helping you. Do not hesitate to ask them. Your reservation will not be held for you after 10:00 p.m. so take care of your bed, check extra gear, deposit extra money---then play. Above all, be sure you know where you are going BEFORE BLACKOUT TIME.

If you lose your return ticket and have no money, go to the R.T.O. at the station. He will issue a warrant to be deducted from your next pay.

WARNING!WARNING!WARNING!

Do NOT buy liquor from a stranger or from anyone other than a good licensed public house.

Beware of bootleggers and cheap private clubs. You may get a knockout drink.

Watch your PASS and PAPERS and do NOT flash a roll of money. Get your bed and check your excess money before you start on a party. A lot of soldiers are getting "rolled" through their own carelessness and lack of caution. All Red Cross Service Clubs have an information service. They will tell you where to go on tours and safe places to go for parties, etc., and can put you in touch with the right kind of people should you wish to accept private invitations.

Do not accept invitations from ANYBODY for ANYTHING in a taproom. Go to a RED CROSS SERVICE CLUB and you'll know its O.K."

The foregoing was good advice for our military personnel. Those who followed it benefited. It would be difficult to measure the outstanding job provided our Armed Forces by the American Red Cross Service Clubs.

One aspect of the war I found very interesting was its effect upon an individual's morale and morals. The British people had been subjected to savage bombings by the German Luftwaffe for a sustained period of time with very devastating results. Each time an allied fighter pilot or bomber crew took off on a combat mission they ran the risk of being shot down. Soldiers training in England knew they would eventually face the enemy in battle and it would be a struggle for them just to survive. Each person had to come to grips with the morale/morals dilemma based upon the degree of influence their

111

participation in the war had placed upon them. This, of course, would vary greatly between individuals for different reasons but primarily based on the urgency of their particular situation.

For instance, an English girl loses a family member to the war and a bomber crew member is scheduled to fly a combat mission the next day. They've only known each other a short time. The night before his mission they become romantically involved and have sex. She didn't know if she would be killed in an air raid later that night. He didn't know if he would survive tomorrow's mission over Germany. What would most young people have done in those circumstances? The morale question came into play along with its short and long term effect on the individual. Again, the extent of degree came into play. Low morale had a rather negative effect resulting in an "I don't care" attitude and conversely, high morale allowed one to be more rational and logical in one's decision-making process.

Prime Minister Winston Churchill did a superb job maintaining a high level of morale for the English people throughout the war. His contribution in this important area went a long way toward winning the war, particularly his passionate and· extraordinary speeches of encouragement.

Leisure was a premium and I was fortunate to get a ticket to see the Bob Hope show at the Odeon Theatre in Leicester Square on 4 July 1943. This was a marvelous show and most appreciated by the GI audience. I saw another great live performance that same year, "This is The Army Mr.Jones" written by Irving Berlin. It starred Mr. Berlin himself with an all-star GI cast. It received wonderful reviews for its run at the famous Palladium Theater. The American couple, Ben Lyons and Bebe Daniels, were established stars in the U. S. before making England their home several years prior to World War II. They enjoyed being the number one radio program on the BBC; quite an honor as television had not yet arrived on the scene. Their show was similar to the Jack Benny and Mary Livingston radio show in the U. S. One Sunday night they did a live show from the lobby of the 32ⁿᵈ M. P. Company, 101 Piccadilly Street. They announced some of our names and hometowns and afterwards provided coffee and cookies for us. We had a delightful time talking with them.

In September 1943 I met Sergeant Mel Ross, 306th Bomb Group, at Rainbow Corner. We became friends. When in London we went out together with our girl friends. I usually dated Joyce. Mel said he would help me transfer into the 306th Bomb Group. He worked in personnel at the time but wanted to be a B-17 gunner.

Wednesday
November 24, 1943
Dear Mother,

Thanks to you all for your swell Christmas presents. They were very useful and worthwhile gifts. I've been trying to get something in the way of Irish linen for you but so far to no avail. Everything is so rationed and coupons required it is very difficult to get something nice. I shall keep trying and know that I will finally get something.

Sorry to hear about Dads accident. Sometimes it takes quite a while for a wound like that to heal. Nearly everyone over here including me has a cold. The usual thing for this time of year.

Yesterday I was at a bomber station seeing about my transfer. The Commanding Officer is putting in a letter of request for me as a Radio Operator/Gunner (B-17). I also have permission at this end to transfer. So I see no reason why it shouldn't go thru this time. I should know within a month. I certainly do hope I make it okay. I'm really crazy about flying and I think I would be of better service in that capacity.

I suppose I've grown a little since you last saw me. I'm 5 ft. 10 inches and weigh 160 pounds. I would fill out much more if I were home. My working hours aren't too healthy. One week I work from 8 PM till 2AM (2nd week), 1PM till 7PM (3rd week) mixed hours. I rotate these duties every week plus inspections, drilling, special duty, etc.

I've met Flight Lieutenant over here from Chattanooga by the name of Kestner from Red Bank and Highland Park. Maybe you might know his family. He's married and about 23 or 24 years old. There is a W.A.C. stationed here from Chattanooga but I haven't met her yet. Her name is Martha Lewis. Do you know her? By the way, I have no use for the W.A.C.s. The ones I've seen or met are snooty and think they are hot stuff, why I don't know because most of the ones I've seen are a bunch of old bags. I would much prefer my English girl friend. Besides, I don't see why they sent them over here in the first place. Those women (you could hardly call them girls) should have relieved men in the states from combat duties overseas and stayed at home where they belong. I hope they don't act at home like they do over here.

We are having a big turkey dinner here tomorrow (Thanksgiving) after services at Westminster Abbey. I'm working all night tonight so won't be able to attend. I shall sleep up to dinnertime.

You said that Jean Hart had written, well I haven't heard from her for well over a year and a half. I would like to hear from her so if you would give her my address and tell her to write I would appreciate it. I would like to write occasionally to one girl at home although I'm not particularly interested in any certain one. I like one and then another. There's no sense in getting serious with one during the war. Things are too uncertain also one might do things here he wouldn't normally in peacetime at home.

"This is the Army" is on its last week here. I was on duty at the theatre and enjoyed the performance very much.

Speaking of that A.W.O.L. Business, well the Officers have forgotten about that. They knew why we went and in a way didn't blame us. They understood how we felt although in their position they recognized it as an Army violation and we were punished accordingly.

The Canadian Army is presenting all of the transferees with the 'Canadian Volunteer Service Medal' and the 'Silver Maple Leaf Cluster' for 18 months active duty. So I will get the ribbon and cluster sometime in December. There isn't anything else to write about so will close now. I love you all very much and I never realized so much before a couple or 3 years ago just how wonderful a Mother I have. No man could ask for anything more. I love you dearly. So long for now.

Love

Jack

After many months submitting my transfer request to the Army Air Force, I realized I was no further ahead than when I started. My objective from the beginning was to comply with Army rules and regulations. Hopefully my request would be granted in due course of time. I wanted to do the right thing from the start but it became apparent I must choose another course of action. However, what choices were available? Then thoughts raced through my mind like déjà vu. Should I risk another Canadian Caper? Should I take the chance of another Courts-Martial to once again tell my story? This would be tricky business at best if my plea did not again fall on sympathetic ears. I consulted with my three compatriots to determine the best course of action for us. These former Canadian soldiers were also disappointed no action had been taken on their transfer requests. They too were ready for a new approach to solve the problem.

After much discussion, we agreed the best approach was to take some action which would result in our being tried at a Special Courts-Martial. Then we would have an opportunity to explain our unique situation. After all, we four soldiers wanted to serve our country in combat action as soon as possible. Our plan gradually developed whereby we would go A.W.O.L.. We would travel to another city and turn ourselves in to the local U. S. Military Police. A nearby city would probably not warrant a court martial. One too far away could result in deep trouble, maybe being labeled as deserters. It was not worth the risk. We finally settled on Belfast, Ireland! This required some careful logistical planning since none of us had ever been to Belfast. We wrote our own official looking orders for travel to Belfast. They stated we were to pick up four U. S. soldiers who had gone A.W.O.L. and return them to their unit in England for disciplinary action. It turned out this was exactly what happened to us.

It took a lot of nerve on our part to conjure up phony orders, proceed to Liverpool where we took a ferryboat across the Irish Sea to Belfast. We did just that, not knowing if our 'papers' were acceptable to make the crossing. Even though we were most apprehensive and somewhat nervous about our daredevil escapade, everything went like clockwork. The four of us always looked sharp in our uniform and our shoes had a 'spit and polish' shine. Amazingly, no one took any interest in us whatsoever. No one really carefully examined our 'orders'. Perhaps there was safety in numbers, too.

We arrived in Belfast, got directions to their largest dance hall, and made our way there with a stop enroute for a bite to eat. Our timing was perfect. The music had just started and there were many unescorted girls. Believe it or not, we even had the moxie to talk to a couple of the U. S. Army M.P.'s who were on duty at the dance hall. They never asked us for our pass or leave papers. Later that night we surrendered to them. They were shocked when we told them what we had done. They took us to their jail where we spent the night.

The next day several Belfast M.P.'s escorted us back to our unit in London. The 32nd M.P. Company commanding officer didn't waste any time preferring court-martial charges against his four wandering boys. Somehow, I had the feeling he wanted to get rid of us. The feeling was mutual. We got what we asked for! Each of us was given an individual Special Courts-Martial trial. I pleaded guilty to the charge and finally had the opportunity to tell my story. I was sentenced as follows: "To be confined at hard labor at such place as the reviewing authority may direct for two (2) months and to forfeit twenty dollars ($20.00) per month for a like period". (A direct quote from the Special-Courts Martial Orders.)

I thought this was a tough sentence and hoped the reviewing authority would reduce it. I was in luck. It was changed from two months hard labor to one-month restriction to my quarters except when performing my duties. The fine remained the same. I was thrilled with the substantial reduction in the sentence. Once again the Lord came to my rescue. Later, I was transferred to the 369th Bomb Squadron, 306th Bomb Group. It finally happened on 12 January 1944. My three friends received similar sentences and were transferred to other units for the Normandy invasion. I never heard from them again.

20. MY NEW HOME—THE 306ᵀᴴ BOMB GROUP

On the afternoon of 12 January 1944, Private Hubbard arrived at the train station in Bedford. The trip from London, almost fifty miles, took about two hours and was uneventful. As the steam train chugged along, I thought about a myriad of things. Could I pass the physical for flying? How would I be accepted? How much training would be required before my first mission? Most of all, how would I feel about flying in combat? I was met at the train station and driven by jeep the five miles or so to my new home, the 306ᵗʰ Bomb Group, near the village of Thurleigh. This was just one of many 8ᵗʰ Air Force bomber bases spread throughout the Midlands area northeast of London. Most of the bases were just a few miles from each other and were very similar in appearance.

January 13, 1944

Dear Mother,

This is the one letter I've been looking forward to writing for months. I was transferred to the 8ᵗʰ Air Force day before yesterday. I'm going in for combat radio operator on Fortresses. I hope to be flying in a month or two.

I've been off of operating for about 8 months. This morning I took a code check at 14 words per minute solid. So with constant practice it shouldn't be hard for me to get back to twenty words a minute.

It has taken nearly a year and a half to get what I've always wanted but it was worth waiting for. I want to do the best I can in my present job and will try to learn all I can.

There are really a swell bunch of fellows here. What a contrast to my former organization! Now I'll be doing a job worthwhile instead of just marking time.

I trust you all are in the best of health and getting along okay. Thanks again for your parcels and letters. I wrote to Jean Hart quite some time ago and haven't heard from her as yet.

Well there isn't much else of interest to write about so will close now hoping to hear from you soon. Please say "hello" to the gang for me.

Love,

Jack

I met Jean Hart at church before the war and had considerable interest in her at the time. We had a budding romance that fizzled out before it really could take off because of our separation during the war years.

The 8th Air Force Bomber Command, code name 'Pinetree', located at High Wycombe, Buckinghamshire, had three air divisions. The First and Third Divisions consisted of B-17 Flying Fortresses and the Second were B-24 Liberators. Bombers from the First Air Division were identified by a large white triangle on the tail of each one. Inside the triangle was a letter of the alphabet, also white, which identified the bomb group. The 306th had an 'H' inside the triangle. The Second Air Division was represented with a circle and the third with a square. Each Air Division had many combat wings. The 40th

Combat Wing (CBW) of the First Air Division consisted of the 92nd, 305th and 306th Bomb Groups. Each Bomb Group had its headquarters, four bomber squadrons, and numerous support units such as Medical, Ordnance, and Maintenance. I was assigned to the 369th Bomb Squadron nicknamed "Fighting Bitin"; whose logo was a bumblebee wearing boxing gloves. The other three squadrons were the 367th "Clay Pigeons", 368th "Eager Beaver", and the 423rd "Grim Reapers".

It was great to see my friend Mel Ross again and be stationed with him. He showed me the main places of interest around the base which helped me get acclimated to my new environment. Mel had left his clerical duties and was the ball turret gunner on Lt. Haywood's crew.

My new living quarters were quite a contrast to my previous palatial home at 101 Piccadilly in London. The six non-commissioned officer members of a crew were not always assigned to the same quarters; sometimes they might be separated. I was assigned to a 'Nissen Hut', which had a large open area with ten double-decker beds on each side. It could accommodate 40 men and had a very small area for toilets; bathing facilities were in another building. Most people bathed only once a week. There was no such thing as deodorant. Collectively, we created a rather pungent smell as it wafted its way through already stale and musty air. This was a fairly standard configuration for all enlisted quarters. The officers weren't much better off. Their single cots making the main difference. Many prisoners incarcerated throughout the U. S. today have much better living conditions than we did while fighting a war; just doesn't seem to make any sense.

There weren't many beds available. I took the top bunk of a bed near one of the two small pot-belly stoves in the building. Since it was winter and miserably cold, I hoped to enjoy a bit of heat from the small stove. I soon learned to feel the heat I had to stand directly beside it.

Sometimes, guys returning from a night at the village pub would drop bullets in to the stove then run to the other end of the building. The exploding bullets sounded like firecrackers and awakened everyone. Most of us took a dim view of this. Luckily no one was injured. As time went by, I managed to gradually get more blankets to ward off the cold. By the time I finished my combat tour I was sleeping under a dozen or more. They kept me warm but I could hardly move under their weight.

21. PREPARING FOR COMBAT

After processing into the 306th I was anxious to complete my training and be assigned to a combat crew. My first order of business was determining my ability to tolerate oxygen satisfactorily in a B-17 at high altitude. If not, my dream of flying for the U. S. Army Air Force would come to an abrupt halt. I anxiously took my first flight ever and after a few hours aloft passed my oxygen test with flying colors. I spent about two weeks getting checked out on the radio equipment, codebooks and other communications training required for a radio-operator/gunner. I easily passed the test for receiving and sending Morse code due to my training and experience while serving in the 32nd M.P. Company and the Canadian Army. I was also taught how to use a parachute, Mae West inflatable life preserver, heated suit, flak vest, oxygen mask and other equipment. I learned how to strip, clean, and use a fifty caliber machine gun, identify both friendly and enemy aircraft by their appearance and silhouette, escape and evade capture and many other things necessary to enhance both safety and survival while defeating the enemy.

There were two types of heated suites. The first was one-piece, similar to long john underwear, light blue in color with metal heating wires throughout except in the bottom, literally. The other was a two-piece khaki-colored Ike (Eisenhower) type jacket, which plugged in to the pants. In both cases gloves and slippers plugged into the suit. The suit had a long cord that plugged into the electrical system of the aircraft. I preferred the two-piece suit; it was more comfortable. Big leather boots went over the slippers and leather gloves went over the heated gloves. At 20,000 to 25,000 feet the temperature got as low as 65 degrees below zero. We always wore heated clothing. The aircraft had two open areas where the left and right waist gunners used 50 caliber machine guns.

When we reached 10,000 feet altitude we put on our oxygen masks. The mask had a long hose, which plugged in to the aircraft oxygen system. Just above the connection was an indicator that blinked each time you breathed, showing whether or not the system was operational.

Located in one corner of the radio operator's compartment was a portable oxygen tank usable for thirty minutes in case of an emergency. The flak jacket was made like a small sandwich board used for advertising. It fit over the front and back of a person and was tied together at the right and left side of the waist. The numerous horizontal metal strips inside the khaki jacket made it very heavy. Most of the time I sat on mine because it was too heavy to wear. Besides, it protected my rump. The steel flak helmet was worn over our leather helmet. I seldom wore it because it was cumbersome and heavy; it reminded me of the gladiators of long ago. In case of emergency or equipment malfunction, we always carried a parachute bag or two that contained spare equipment, gloves, shoes, and jackets. Spare equipment was used more than once during my tour of missions.

The pilot and co-pilot wore backpack parachutes. The navigator, and bombardier engineer, radio operator/gunner, ball turret gunner, left and right waist gunners and the tail gunner wore a harness. The parachute buckled on to the front of the harness. It was called a chest parachute. The yellow colored Mae West life jacket was worn under the parachute harness. It was yellow so it could be easily identified in the water and was inflated by pulling two handles that caused it to rapidly inflate automatically. If this didn't work, you could blow air into a rubber tube and manually inflate it much the same as those used on aircraft today.

I took my training very seriously. It was truly a cram course. I went so far as to practice running from my radio compartment to the plane's rear door in case I had to bail out. I was looking for speed and timed myself. I could do it in seven seconds. I had a tremendous amount to learn in a short time. Individual crewmembers had been trained in the U. S. to become proficient in their particular area of expertise. Afterwards, they were assigned to a crew and continued training together. After many months of training and when judged combat-ready, crews were assigned overseas. I believe training and discipline is very important. We can make mistakes in training and correct them but mistakes in combat are usually fatal. When crewmembers were wounded or killed replacements were assigned. I was a replacement radio operator/gunner without the extensive training, crew integrity and longtime togetherness other crews experienced. Sometimes I felt like an outcast.

22. MY FIRST MISSION

It finally happened! On 29 January 1944, after only 16 days in the 306th Bomb Group, I was scheduled to fly my first combat mission - the second time I had ever flown. There was a good chance of being shot down and bailing out over enemy territory; therefore I was promoted to sergeant because the Germans treated NCO prisoners of war better than enlisted men—a comforting thought!

The descriptions of combat missions in this book are taken mainly from Headquarters 306th Bomb Group Intelligence Reports. These reports were written immediately after completion of each mission and from my own personal experiences. Some references are made to the publication 369th Bomb Squadron Combat Diary 1942—1945, authored by Wiley W. Glass, Allan B. Richardson, John M. Kavanaugh and Henry L. P. Moore; compiled by Russell A. Strong. Strong also wrote the excellent book, First Over Germany, a history of the 306th Bombardment Group.

As always, we were summoned by the squadron charge of quarters (CQ). He opened the door of our Nissen hut about 2:30 a.m., turned on the lights, yelled out the names of the pilots scheduled for missions that day and specified the amount of fuel for the mission. Fuel indicated the approximate length of the mission, which gave us some idea of the possible general location of the target. Only those crewmembers called got up out of a warm bed to face the uncertainty of the day. Since I was a replacement, he called out my name and identified my pilot, Lt. Alvin Schuering, whom I did not know. Breakfast was at 3:15 a.m. followed by our classified mission briefing at 4:15 a.m.

A truck took us to the mess hall. A few diehards walked or rode their bikes. It was miserably cold. Especially when the wind was blowing. Rain was common in this part of the country often causing what seemed like seas of mud. More often than not we could count on the famous English fog to cover us like a blanket. Sometimes so thick visibility was almost nil. The local weather at takeoff time had little bearing, if any, on whether a mission would proceed as scheduled. It depended primarily upon the projected weather conditions over the target.

I've never forgotten our breakfast. We had poorly cooked powdered eggs floating in water and not too appetizing. After breakfast we went to the Group briefing room where our crews and key brass assembled. The commanding officer spoke briefly followed by the Operations and Intelligence officers and the curtain parted. It showed a huge map of the British Isles, France, Germany and most of northern Europe. Colored yarn represented the route to be flown from our base to the primary target, Frankfurt, and the return route to our base. The map provided other essential information including take-off times, place of departure from the English coast and various altitudes to be flown. It showed the time we should be at certain points along the route. The group navigator performed an important function whereby everyone would set their GI watch, called a 'hack' watch, at a given hour and minute. It was a count-down and when the second hand was at 12 everyone pushed in the stem of the watch as the navigator yelled 'hack'. It was very important that everyone had the exact same time down to the second. Other officers briefed us where to expect enemy fighters and flak, along with communications, fighter support, bomb load, alternate targets, weather, and other pertinent information.

After the briefing we went to our squadron supply room and were issued our flight clothing, equipment, and escape and evasion kit. The kit contained currency of European countries, a map, compass, and our passport photo in civilian clothes, a jacket, shirt, and tie. The underground partisans who helped allied airmen escape capture and return to England used these items. Trucks took crews to their aircraft. We went to our aircraft; tail number L-953, located on the hardstand just off the taxiway. Hardstands were located around the perimeter of the base. The ground crew was located in a small tent, which housed other items such as 50 caliber machine guns and ammunition. Boxes of additional ammunition were beside our gun positions in the aircraft. I can't say enough for the wonderful job that our ground crews did keeping our aircraft in tip-top shape. They were dedicated and excelled at their jobs. After we took off on a mission they sweated out our return along with others. They were really special! We inspected the aircraft exterior and then climbed aboard our bomber, went to our respective positions and checked out everything to make sure it was operational. Each of us had a small box lunch. It usually contained two sandwiches and some chocolate fudge candy. By the time we had an opportunity to eat, the food was frozen and curled up. After it thawed, I tried to eat as much as I could because I was really hungry. It was a long time between breakfast at 3:15 a.m. and returning from this mission around 2:30 p.m. We were always debriefed immediately after returning and that meant another hour or so before eating.

23. UP, UP AND AWAY

There was a scheduled time to start engines, warm and check them out. At the direction of the control tower, each plane taxied out (we were scheduled at 7:25 a.m.) to their designated position ready for take-off (ours was scheduled for 7:40 a.m.). Aircraft took off one after the other spaced about one minute apart. As we roared down the runway, loaded with twelve 500 pound high explosive bombs and maximum fuel, our weight caused the aircraft to strain a bit to get off the ground. She lifted off and began her climb through thick gray black overcast skies like the valiant lady she was.

Every takeoff during my tour of missions was an unnerving experience for me praying steadily through each one. I guess I felt that way after the misfortune one dark morning seeing a plane ahead of us go down the runway and crash on takeoff. It blew up. Everyone lost his life. I didn't mind landings but conditions for takeoff could be bad. Climbing through thousands of feet of solid overcast skies breaking out from cloud cover to start forming our bombers into squadron and group formations was a rather exciting experience. Sometimes terrifying.

On another mission, climbing through overcast skies, we flew through a B-24 formation. Our pilot told us to look for B-24s and let him know their location relative to our aircraft should he need to take immediate corrective action. We were flying toward 12 o'clock and I saw a B-24 flying from nine o'clock towards three o'clock maybe 20 feet below us. All this happened in seconds like a flash. If a crash was imminent, there was not enough time to prevent an accident. This sort of thing causes your heart to beat a little faster as you gulp for air.

During the war, the 8th Air Force had over 350,000 men assigned to just over 100 Bomber and Fighter bases in England. Over 6,500 aircraft of all types were lost and

4,000 plus were damaged. 8th Air Force airmen claimed over 11,481 enemy aircraft shot down and more than 4,200 destroyed on the ground. 26,000 airmen were killed, many wounded and over 28,000 were prisoners of war. Fourteen airmen were decorated with the Medal of Honor, which was almost half of the total awarded to USAAF personnel in World War II. The 8th Air Force was never once turned back by the enemy. Wartime combat is definitely for young men. Almost all of our flyers were between the ages of 18 and 25. Many of us didn't realize the extent of the danger we faced. Each man could expect to complete only eight missions or only one in three would complete their 25 missions. Not even a 50-50 chance! I'm glad I didn't know this startling bit of news until after the war. It was a job we had to do. Everyone was committed to defeat the enemy. That didn't mean we weren't scared; no doubt we were. However, we had total confidence in our leaders, our training, and the magnificent B-17 aircraft.

Finally, our group was in formation heading for our target, Frankfurt, Germany. At 8:30 a.m. while still over England we put on our oxygen masks and started using oxygen as we reached 10,000 feet altitude. We were just one group in a stream of many groups usually organized into wings heading for Nazi Germany to drop bombs on various assigned targets. This must have been an awesome sight to view from the ground as wave after wave of American bombers flew across Germany in the daylight. It was a clear, beautiful day and I could see for miles as one bomber formation followed another. It truly was an amazing spectacle. Royal Air Force (RAF) Stirling, Lancaster, and Mosquito bombers attacked German targets at night after Americans bombed Germany during the day. We were scheduled to have fighter support—American P-47 Thunderbolts, P-38 Lightnings, P-51 Mustangs and RAF Spitfires—from the enemy coast to the bombing run and back out again. Often times there were gaps between our fighter escort aircraft and our bombers. German fighters relished this opportunity. They would pounce upon our unprotected bombers usually wreaking disaster on our bombers and crews.

Prior to entering enemy territory, at a little past 10:00 a.m., our pilot gave the order to 'test fire' our guns. This meant each person manning a gun fired several short bursts of ammunition out into the wild blue yonder to make sure they operated properly. Suffice it to say, we were careful not to hit one of our own nearby bombers although it did happen more than once. The burst of fire from the twin guns in the top turret near me made an unbelievably loud sound. Hearing it the first time was nerve wracking. I flinched momentarily. As time went by, it became routine. I never became completely accustomed to the 'rat-ta-tat' exploding sound of the .50 caliber machine gun bullets.

24. FLYING OVER ENEMY TERRITORY

The 306th had 43 aircraft on this mission. We flew in the low squadron of the lead Group led by Major Robert Riordan, 369th Bomb Squadron Commanding Officer. At 9:45 a.m. one B-17 was seen smoking and going down through the clouds about half way to the English channel, apparently out of control. The following aircraft aborted the mission as follows: Pilot Bill Hilton, 369th Squadron, turned back midway over the channel at 9:58 a.m. due to internal failure of #2 engine; Pilot Floyd Brunn, 368th Squadron turned back just past Liege, Belgium about 35 miles over enemy territory due to internal failure of #4 engine supercharger; Pilot Ted Czechowski, 369th Squadron, turned back over England after gyro compass and artificial horizon became inoperative and the aircraft went into spiral spin. His right waist gunner bailed out when aircraft temporarily went out of control and later returned to the base, as did all the remaining aircraft.

One of my jobs was monitoring our 8th Air Force radio station in England, whose call sign was 7MT. The station frequently identified itself by transmitting its call sign in Morse code. The call sign translated into da da dit dit dit for the number 7, da da for the letter M and da for T. It was done on a pre-assigned AM frequency. These signals were sent at predetermined times which gave radio operators the opportunity to keep their radio receivers (BC-348-R) properly tuned to the transmitting station. The enemy would sometimes try to imitate and or jam 7MT but met with little success. It was important to be alert for any transmissions that could effect the mission in progress.

During one mission I received a message repeating the encoded letters RA KM. When decoded, using the list of double letters from my classified code list for this particular mission it read, "Abandon mission—Return to base". Additionally, the transmitted message was authenticated to make sure it was a genuine message from our headquarters. One radio operator in each formation was assigned the position of 'lead radio operator'. He manned his radio throughout the mission; however, the pilot could cut in with voice communications on the intercom as needed. The radio operator did not use his machine gun during this time. Other radio operators were assigned back up in case something happened to the lead operator.

Toward the end of my tour of missions I flew lead radio operator occasionally. I didn't like this assignment because I couldn't hear conversations on our plane's intercom system. Nor could I see what was happening outside the aircraft because I was operating the radio. When enemy aircraft attacked us, I wanted to listen on the intercom so I would know which direction they were coming from and how many. I also wanted to know when we were approaching flak so the thunderous explosions would not surprise me. When unexpected, it felt like you would jump out of your skin! As it happened, I winced and could immediately see my oxygen indicator blinking more rapidly than normal. Quickly, I settled back into my usual routine, if you could call it that, realizing the impending danger was the exploding flak.

Although I had a window by my radio position and another one on the opposite side of the plane, my overall vision outside the aircraft was limited. Just below the window was a 'chaff' chute used for throwing chaff outside the aircraft. Chaff consisted of a bundle of metal strips about 12 inches long by a one-quarter inch wide and looked like a sturdier version of Christmas tree tinsel. There were about 100 strips in a bundle. When directed by the Navigator I would start throwing out 150 bundles spaced a few seconds apart. Chaff was used to jam enemy radar reducing the effectiveness of their anti-aircraft firepower. Only specified aircraft in a formation were designated to drop chaff. This provided maximum coverage and effectiveness. The Germans used radar for various reasons but primarily to determine the height, speed, and other data about our aircraft. This allowed their anti-aircraft guns to zero-in on us more accurately. When Germans saw chaff on their ground radarscopes, it must have looked like a blizzard as it floated to earth.

Certain aircraft in our formation carried large cameras (K-20) which were used to photograph the target after "bombs away". These photos were used to evaluate bombing effectiveness. Aircraft with cameras were selected for their location in the flight formation so maximum photo coverage would be assured. The camera was housed in a camera well located in the underside of the aircraft several feet below and a couple of feet to the right of the radio operator's position. During one mission while carrying a camera an 88MM shell exploded under it. Shrapnel flew in every direction. A piece about three inches long and one-half inch wide lodged just under my seat while flying as lead radio operator. The camera and other equipment deflected the shrapnel direction from the blast. It may have saved me from injury or death. I felt very fortunate we carried a camera that day.

During one mission our bomb bay was loaded with propaganda leaflets called 'Nickels' by the British. We dropped thousands of them over the target. I saved one, which I still have. They were single sheets of paper, eight and one-half inches by five inches. On one side was the heading, "Wie Deutschland noch gerettet werden?". A loose translation is, "Germany can still be saved." On the reverse in large bold print it read "Wenn Friede Einkehrt", meaning, "When peace comes back". One side was printed in black and gray and the other side in black and red with the words filling both sides. When scheduled, only one aircraft in our group carried propaganda leaflets on a bombing mission.

There were basically two types of flak; tracking and barrage. Tracking occurred when anti-aircraft batteries fired their shells directly in the path of an aircraft. The Germans hoped their radar and other calculations were accurate causing shells to explode at a predetermined time and altitude, destroying the incoming aircraft. Barrage occurred when the Germans fired numerous flak guns covering an area, which they expected our bombers to fly through. For example, our formations might be flying at altitudes between 21,000 and 25,000 feet; hence, the enemy would try to box the bombers in between these altitudes firing their 88MM guns at various heights within a box hoping to down as many bombers as possible.

When our aircraft reached the initial point (IP) of the bomb run, the pilot gave control of the plane to the bombardier. He flew it directly to the target using his controls. This straight flight at the same altitude usually lasted from 10 to 30 minutes and was extremely dangerous. When flying through flak during this time the pilot could not take evasive action to avoid being hit. As soon as the bombs were released on the target, the bombardier would say "Bombs away" on the intercom and the pilot took control taking evasive action as needed to dodge the flak. I was afraid of the impending flak because of the very loud, rapid 'boom, boom, boom, boom, boom' sound it made as it exploded nearby. It sent varying sized pieces of steel shrapnel in every direction accompanied by huge puffs of black smoke. A direct hit could cause extreme damage or put an end to what started out as a good day. As soon as I heard "Bombs away" on the intercom it was my duty to immediately open the door from my radio compartment to the bomb bay and visually check that all bombs were dropped, then tell the pilot on the intercom "Bomb bay all clear". Sometimes, pieces of shrapnel would hit different parts of the plane, causing varying degrees of damage. If

I had a choice, I'd choose fighter attack anytime over flak. I never changed my mind about this throughout my missions. I believed my chances for survival were greater with fighter attacks than flak.

Canadian Army Trooper—1940

Black Puffs of Flak

B-17 On Fire

Bombs Away

Bombs Exploding

Jack C. Hubbard

Classic Crash Landing

Returned to Base With Death and Destruction

More Death and Destruction

Jack On Right With OCS Military Award

25. THESE ARE REAL BULLETS

So far so good, I thought. As we approached our target, an industrial center in Frankfurt, everything seemed to be going okay. Since I had no experience, I really didn't have a clue whether it was or not; or even what to expect. As we approached our bombing run there was intense flak. To make matters worse, there was a gap in our fighter support between the end of P-47 fighter cover and arrival of P-38 fighter cover. As we started our bomb run at 11:03 a.m. all hell broke loose! Twenty-five enemy aircraft, both single engine Messerschmidt 109s (ME-109s) and Fock-Wulfe 190s (FW-190s), and twin engine Junkers 88s (JU-8s) attacked us for six minutes. Being my first mission, I didn't realize the losses that could be inflicted on aircraft and crews in a very short period of time. I later learned the tragic consequences.

We bombed our target at 11:09 a.m. Fighter support was again absent from 11:15 a.m. to 11:30 a.m. resulting in further attacks. All attacks were from the tail. Three JU-88s and three FW-190s attacked the low group twice on the bombing run, both types firing rockets from as close as 150 yards. At least two rockets burst between the aircraft in our formation. Fortunately, these rockets did not cause any damage. Our crews claimed two JU-88s destroyed and one damaged, along with one FW 190 destroyed in this encounter. At 11:15 a.m. about 10 to 15 JU-88s, ME-109s and FW-190s made similar attacks for 15 minutes. Ferocious and fierce air battles took place in a matter of minutes causing much death and destruction.

On missions I flew all crewmembers worked hard doing the job they were trained to do. We didn't have time to think about anything else. I never witnessed any panic or emotional disturbance during combat. We were fighting for survival. I believe every man performed at optimum levels. Intercom conversation between crewmembers was usually in a calm voice unless it was to get the crew's immediate attention when enemy fighters attacked us or witnessing one of our B-17's taking a hit. Then we would yell, "Bail out! Bail out!" to that crew as if that would help them. Sometimes they made it out; sometimes they didn't. When a plane was shot down, we did our best to identify it by tail number, number of chutes, and any additional information we observed. B-17s in distress were called 'hot news' and given to our intelligence officer during debriefing after the mission. It was very painful for us to watch our buddies go down, especially when only a few or no parachutes were seen. Worst yet were those young men who went down in flames or their planes blew up with no hope of survival. Still, we had to carry on and hopefully live through the engagement to fight another day.

In the foregoing air battle, 306th bombers claimed one JU88 and one ME 109 destroyed. No planes were lost during this engagement with the Luftwaffe or from "ack ack" fire as the anti-aircraft guns were called. At 11:09 a.m. we saw a B-17 from another group going down in flames. There were no chutes. Two purple rockets fired from the ground burst to one side of our formation and one red flare burst after bombs away. These may have been signals to Luftwaffe fighters from their ground personnel. After "Bombs Away" our pilot took evasive action to dodge the heavy flak as we flew toward England. Several flak batteries fired at us as we flew over Germany. Fortunately they were poor shots. Eventually we flew in brilliant sunshine at 23,000 feet homeward bound. I was so happy to get back to our base without a scratch or injury to anyone in our crew. It was true that often an easy mission for some crews could be a rough one for others. As we approached our base, a 368th plane fired red flares (from a Verey pistol) into the air, signifying wounded men on board. This alerted the medics and gave that aircraft first priority to land.

We landed at 2:27 p.m. Trucks were waiting to take us directly to debriefing by our intelligence officers. Every crew was debriefed in great detail after each mission. These classified reports were compiled, typed, and sent to the commanding officer and higher headquarters as soon as possible the same day. Each plane was inspected for damage and the report included:

367th Squadron: 8 Not Damaged
SEVERE DAMAGE: A/C 726 with 20MM left and right inner wings and tail component. 2 Bulkheads hit by flak

368th Squadron: 2 Not Damaged
5 Slight Damage
SEVERE DAMAGE: A/C 454 with vertical/dorsal fin and rudder damaged by .50 caliber fire; A/C 363 right outer wing hit by flak.

369th Squadron: 5 Not Damaged
2 Slight Damage
SEVERE DAMAGE: A/C 056 with flak damage to left horizontal stabilizer and ball turret, flak entering turret causing internal damage, left landing light and number 3 oil cooler damaged by empty .50 caliber shell cases

423rd Squadron: 10 Not Damaged
2 Slight Damage

After debriefing, both officers and NCOs went to the food line. First we were offered a jigger or more of good quality liquor. Steaks and eggs were cooked to order. Other meat, vegetables, and desserts were available on the food line. It was like a visit to a cafeteria. The ice cream plant serving the surrounding airfields was located on our base. We made the most of it and stuffed ourselves on ice cream. I usually had a steak with six real fried eggs on top with all the 'trimmings'. What a contrast to the powdered eggs we had for breakfast. I would have preferred real eggs before the mission instead of afterwards. I wondered about this and had a bizarre thought. Eggs were hard to come by. Maybe they wouldn't have to feed as many people real eggs after a mission because of our losses.

After landing from a mission, our ground crews were busy repairing and replacing parts on the damaged planes. Those bombers needed to be airworthy as soon as possible, hopefully for the next mission. Our men worked long hours, sometimes around the clock to get the job done. I believed they displayed remarkable skill, ingenuity, tenaciousness, and a commitment and dedication to duty seldom found anywhere today. I greatly admired and appreciated each one of them.

About half of our B-17s had names with caricatures and other forms of art painted on the front of the plane near the nose. Some of the 369th names were: FICKLE FINGER, EXTRA JOKER, SLEEPY TIME GAL, HOW SOON, SONS OF FURY, JOAN OF ARC, FOUR OF A KIND, LITTLE AUDREY, DAMYANKEE, SILVER STREAK, PICCADILLY COMMANDO, MISS CARRIAGE, CAPT'N AND HIS KIDS, MISS AMERICA, and LIBERTY BELLE. I never flew on a plane with a name.

On 29 January 1944 the Group completed its 103rd mission since 9 October 1942. I now had one mission under my belt with 24 more to go. Oddly enough, I didn't think about it that way nor did most of the other men. We were living in the present, not the past or the future. Consciously or subconsciously we were committed to living one day at a time and living it to the fullest. We realized the dangers ahead but didn't dwell on them and rarely talked about it. There was great camaraderie among us. We had a positive attitude; good sense of humor, helped and supported each other when needed. Every man knew the importance of winning this war. He realized it was truly a life or death matter for the survival of our Republic and the American way of life. We knew everyone back home was totally behind the war effort and us. That support was very important and appreciated. Everyone knew we would win the war. We just didn't know when. We were confident of victory because God was on our side. I wonder if the Germans thought the same. Probably.

26. MY SECOND MISSION

I wondered how long I would wait before my next mission. I didn't have too long to think about it. I was called the next day, 30 January, and again flew with pilot Lt. Schuering on aircraft 953-L. We bombed aircraft production at Brunswick, Germany. Enemy opposition was slight and no claims were made for shooting down Luftwaffe aircraft. The Group lost no aircraft and the 369th did not even receive any flak damage. However, it was a difficult day because of poor visibility. Haze and vapor trails strained the nerves of everyone. Two B-17s of the 92nd Group collided in the target area killing both crews. There were other aircraft in distress at different times. If you could call any combat mission an easy one for the 369th, this was it. We called this kind of mission a 'milk run'! It would be nice if all of them were like this but that was truly wishful thinking.

The London News Chronicle, Monday, January 31, 1944, stated Saturday's assault on Frankfurt, the greatest in air war history, cost the Luftwaffe 102 fighters. Allied losses totaled 31 bombers and 13 fighters. The raid on Brunswick and Hannover cost the USAAF 18 bombers and five fighters. The Luftwaffe losses were 91 fighters. The headlines from the Sunday London Times said, "Over 800 U. S. Heavies Hit Frankfort By Day". This was the greatest number of bombers yet sent out of Britain by the United States Army Air Force. It had an escort of fighters, etc.

It usually took about five or six months to complete the required 25 combat missions because raids weren't scheduled every day, no unit was scheduled for every mission flown by the 8th Air Force, the number of air-worthy planes varied, and crews needed rest between missions to prevent combat fatigue. When not flying a mission we attended daily squadron meetings and various training classes. Training included enemy aircraft identification, skeet shooting (trapshooting whereby clay targets were quickly thrown in such a way as to simulate the angles of a flight of birds) and escape and evasion. Visiting our War Room and reading classified intelligence reports was interesting and informative. I did so much skeet shooting I got tired of it, especially in the bitter, cold weather. Skeet shooting was supposed to improve our gunnery skills. I identified so many German aircraft silhouettes I saw them in my sleep.

I enjoyed the escape and evasion training. Particularly when the speaker was an actual evadee. Several airmen told how they made it out of Germany and back to England. There were fascinating stories about their experiences with members of the partisan underground. A sergeant from our group was on a paint detail in a POW camp, painting the center stripe down the middle of the street. When he got to the main gate, he kept on painting outside of the camp. No one paid any attention to him; he made a run for it and was able to evade re-capture. Later, he reached a partisan group who helped him through enemy territory and eventually back to England. What an exciting experience!

Some of our on-going training was airborne. We fired our guns at targets towed by one of our B-17's. Fortunately no one hit the tow plane. The most important training was learning to fly a 'tight' formation. When all aircraft in a formation flew close as practical to each other, maximum firepower could be directed at enemy fighters. This was very serious business because while flying in formation over enemy territory, Luftwaffe fighters would usually fly alongside one bomber group after another, just out of range of our machine gun fire, looking for loose formations to attack. They would concentrate their efforts making fierce attacks on those poor guys. Stragglers hardly had a chance. Checking the stream of bombers, looking for weak formations usually paid off big dividends for Hitler's airmen. Colonel Curtis E. LeMay was Executive Officer of the 306th early in the war. He later devised the stacking and spacing of aircraft whereby maximum firepower could be achieved against enemy fighters. Without this technique, daylight bombing would have been prohibitive because of excessive loss of manpower and aircraft. After the war, LeMay became a four-star general and for a number of years was Commander of the USAF Strategic Air Command, a major deterrent against the USSR during the cold war. He later became Chief of Staff of the USAF. Our future survival now, as then, is dependent upon 'Peace through Strength'.

27. DOWELL'S CREW

Several days after bombing Frankfurt we were shown photographs of the results. We were told the damage was so devastating we would not have to go back any time soon. Soon came quickly. On 4 February we hit Frankfurt again. I was now permanently assigned to Lt. Kenneth Dowell's crew and happy to finally be a member of a team but not happy about the circumstances which placed me there.

On 11 January 1944, Dowell's crew bombed the huge aircraft factory at Halberstadt, Germany. Heavy resistance was experienced. Overwhelming German fighter attacks lasted for an hour. During one onslaught, about 40 FW 190s in desperate head on attacks succeeded in knocking down five 306th bombers. Forty-three of their 50 crewmembers were killed. This was one of the highest one-day personnel losses ever experienced by the Group. German fighters shot up all 27 remaining aircraft. Many were also hit by flak. Most of the difficulty was attributed to lack of allied fighter support. No one adequately explained their absence. Unexpected bad weather may have prevented some of the fighters from getting off the ground. But all of them? On top of this our problems were further compounded because our base at Thurleigh was closed due to bad weather. All the returning 306th planes were diverted to eight other bases.

It was a very bad day! Dowell's number three engine was hit but he was able to feather it. It caught on fire. Dowell put the plane into a dive. Flames streaming out of the mangled engine burned so furiously it fell off the plane. Dowell said that probably saved them. As they were in the dive a Luftwaffe ME-109 flew along with them spraying the crippled plane with machine gun fire. With the electrical system shot out, Dowell hit the alarm bell for the crew to bail out. It didn't work. No one bailed out.

151

Dowell regained control of the aircraft as it leveled off at 4,000 feet. It was a real challenge to fly. Later, when some of the crew-members could check the damage, they found the landing gear inoperative, several control cables were shot away and the horizontal stabilizer was loosened by the dive and machine gun fire. The aircraft continued but was very difficult to fly; the oxygen system was gone, the top turret was inoperable and the tail wheel would not go down. Dowell's plane was one of the flying 'wounded' as it staggered all the way back to England. Sadly, there were five wounded crewmembers aboard. The bombardier had a severe leg would and the radio operator had serious head and arm wounds. A shell had exploded in the top turret, causing the plexiglas to shatter, spraying tiny bits into the engineers face; one waist gunner was hit in his rear end and the tail gunner was hit on the top of his hands. The bombardier and radio operator were eventually sent to the U.S. because of their serious wounds. The other three men returned to duty within three to four weeks.

Dowell barely made it back to England and crash-landed at Great Saling, an RAF station. This was the end of 'Pretty Baby' as she was called. The plane was declared a total loss. Because of his exceptional flying skill and his many other accomplishments bringing the plane and crew back to England, Lt. Dowell was awarded one of the highest U. S. Military decorations, the Silver Star. His co-pilot, Lt. Young, received the Distinguished Flying Cross for his flying skills. Each of the wounded crewmembers received the Purple Heart for their combat wounds.

I considered myself fortunate to be on Dowell's crew because of his past combat experience and exceptional flying ability. He was a real 'cool customer' in extreme adverse situations. He had a good, seasoned combat crew who had truly experienced their 'baptism of fire' with the enemy. Mel Ross, flying with Lt. Gerald

Haywood, started out on this mission, but returned to base early because of mechanical difficulties, as did Lt. Czechowski. Mel and I had two-day passes to London waiting for us after we completed this mission. Soon as we reached enemy territory on this, my third mission, we encountered a great deal of anti-aircraft fire all along the route to our target in Frankfurt. In the vicinity of Bonn, two barrages were laid down forcing all the aircraft in our formation to fly into a corridor, leaving little room for evasive action. The corridor was filled with very accurate tracking anti-aircraft gunfire. At Frankfurt the ack ack was exceptionally accurate and with great intensity. Lt. Charles Berry, 367th Squadron, was hit by flak in the right wing and the plane burst into flames. It went into a spin and eventually broke in half at the ball turret. The front of the aircraft went down, killing everyone in that section. The tail section stabilized long enough for three crewmembers to bail out.

Just after dropping our bombs we were hit by flak in number one engine, knocking it out. Great black puffs of smoke from flak were all around us. It seemed we were being swallowed by it. Like a big black hole, we flew through it with only small flak holes in the aircraft. Amazingly, the damage was minor. As we left the target we tried to keep up with our formation with our three good engines. It was hopeless. The 306th gradually faded away from view. It was a beautiful day. Clear as a bell. Suddenly, I realized we were all alone flying across Germany; a sitting duck to be picked off at will by a German fighter. I started thinking about my pass to London that awaited me. It wasn't looking too promising at the moment. We shot flares from our very pistol, signaling 'help' to any friendly fighters who might be in our vicinity hoping they would see us and come to our temporary rescue.

Soon the unexpected happened! Four P-47s with the markings 'HL' (78th Fighter Group) spotted us. Realizing

153

our plight they swooped down out of the blue towards our crippled B-17. Two of them lowered their flaps and wheels to slow their speed and one flew on each side of us. They were very close to us. It was easy to distinguish the pilots as they waved to us. Even though short lived, it was a moving experience at such a critical time. Our prayers were answered! Overall, fighter support was excellent flying both to and from the target. On the way home, Lt. Henry Ware, 369th Squadron, was shot down near Calais on the French coast. All the crew bailed out and everyone survived. I later learned the German ack ack gunners around the Pas de Calais area were all 'sharp shooters'. These guys must have been the highest-ranking sergeants with extensive experience. All of them were expert marksmen. I hated to fly anywhere near those flak guns. They were so dangerous! After crossing the water Dowell started letting down, arriving the English coast at Margate. We landed at our base at 4:14 p.m., 57 minutes late. We were fortunate not to have encountered one single German fighter plane. Amazing.

At one point in our string of missions, some of the 8th Air Force gunners took their 50 caliber machine guns out of their mounts as soon as they reached the English coast. Consequently, there would be less work to do when they landed. This practice came to a screeching halt one day when German fighters followed a group toward their base and shot down a B-17. The unprepared gunners couldn't defend themselves. Too bad the change wasn't instituted earlier.

Earlier during the intelligence de-briefing other crews said we had gone down; therefore, everyone was surprised to see our happy, smiling faces. As soon as I could, I made a beeline to pick up my pass and head for London. I arrived at the Universal Brasserie around 9 p.m. as Mel and some of my other buddies were toasting their comrade in arms, Jack, who was shot down that day. You should have seen their faces when they saw me. Was it a ghost? Or, had they had one too many? Soon their faces were filled with joy when they knew it really was me. It was a night of celebration. I was thankful to be alive.

Joyce had previously made an appointment for Mel and me to have our photographs taken for our families. They turned out okay...didn't show the results of our night on the town. The next night Joyce and I along with Mel and his date went dancing at Covent Garden. We had a wonderful time together and completely oblivious to the war for several fun-filled hours. Before I returned to my base, Joyce and I had a rather serious discussion. We previously talked about marriage. Because of my uncertain future flying combat missions, we agreed to wait until I had completed them.

28. BETWEEN COMBAT MISSIONS

Sixteen days passed before I flew my next mission. During the breaks between missions we participated in further training. Sometimes we flew weather missions in a stripped down B-17 collecting data and reporting weather conditions to headquarters. I didn't care for these weather flights; the conditions we flew through were terrible and sometimes frightening. It just wasn't my cup of tea. These flights and towing targets didn't count as combat missions. Most of us felt if we were going to fly, we would rather fly where it counted, toward completing our 25 missions. However, someone had to do it. Luckily for me it didn't happen often. On one weather scouting flight, I overheard the pilot and co-pilot, neither of whom I had ever flown with, talking on the intercom. The pilot said he thought he could loop the stripped B-17. The copilot didn't think he should try it. I started to break out in a sweat and buckled on my parachute. I was out of there in a flash if they decided to do something that stupid! They discussed it for a while and the pilot gave into reason. He vowed to try it some day. I wonder if he ever did it.

All crew-members were required to attend daily meetings in our 369th Combat Operations Room. Our Squadron Commander and First Sergeant would cover important matters for our information. Medals were awarded at this time. An Air Medal was awarded each man who completed five combat missions. After receiving the first medal an oak leaf cluster was given in lieu of another medal, representing subsequent awards. Flyers fortunate enough to finish 25 missions were awarded the Distinguished Flying Cross and usually returned to the U.S. and their loved ones.

As a point of interest, combat crews wore a blue cloth patch about three and one-half inches by one and one-half inches under their wings on their uniform jacket. This identified these airmen as combat flyers.

29. BIG WEEK

For a successful invasion of Western Europe, the Combined Chiefs of Staff declared it was absolutely essential the German Air Force be completely destroyed or rendered ineffective both in the air and on the ground. This included aircraft production. The major attack to meet this objective was originally scheduled to begin on 11 February 1944, but was delayed until 20 February due to bad flying weather. 'Big Week', as the assault was called, was a maximum effort. An all out attack on German fighters in the air and on the ground. Aircraft production facilities and fuel depots were targeted as well. At the time, I was not aware this assault was called 'Big Week'. I suppose only the 'top brass' knew about it because it was highly classified information. To me these missions were just part of a string of missions and I never realized the significance of them at the time. The veteran 306ᵗʰ was counted on for its usual high performance during this period and they didn't let anyone down.

On 20 February the target was Leipzig, Germany. The 306ᵗʰ lost one aircraft, Lt. Harold Richard, 423ʳᵈ, due to flak crippling an engine. He was knocked out of the formation in the target area and German fighters attacked the damaged plane. He was killed along with a waist gunner; the rest of the crew bailed out safely but were captured. One thousand U. S. bombers and 1,000 U. S. fighters participated in this mission. Finally, the Americans were attacking the enemy in great strength. I still marvel at the planning and logistics required to successfully launch 2,000 aircraft and crews for a single daylight raid on well defended enemy targets.

My fourth mission on 21 February was the primary target at Lippstadt, Germany, but the weather made visual identification of the target impossible. We did not have a Pathfinder aircraft equipped with radar to identify the target; therefore, we bombed our secondary target, which was an airdrome located at Hopsten. Later, strike photos showed we missed the airfield but did one heck of a job plowing up a farmer's field. There was a fierce attack on the Group ahead of us and our fighter support went to their aid. During a ten-minute lull in fighter support the 306th underwent a head on attack by two ME-210s. Fortunately no planes were lost and everyone escaped injury. Mel flew with Lt. Haywood and we were in the same seven-plane formation. We were separated by one plane. Moderate but accurate ack ack fire was encountered at the coast both going in and coming out of the target. Out of the group's 21 aircraft which flew the mission more than half were damaged by flak, five seriously, but all returned with no personnel casualties.

The 8th Air Force maximum effort continued with the 306th in the sky once again with 39 aircraft on 22 February. Nine planes aborted the mission before reaching the target and did not drop their bombs. We were one of those planes; due to mechanical trouble we returned to the base early. I really disliked having to abort a mission after going through all the preparation, flying through the soup to form up, continuing with the Group towards the target and then having to turn back for various reasons. Mel again flew with Lt. Haywood. This time the target was a big JU-88 aircraft plant at Bernburg, Germany. Later our intelligence reports indicated the bomb damage slowed aircraft production by 70 to 80 percent during the following month.

Just after the target was bombed, the P-51 support escort vanished. Twenty ME-109s attacked our Group. Soon several P-51s appeared and drove the enemy away without any losses to the 306th. Near Koblenz the P-51 escort left again leaving the Group unprotected. Shortly thereafter, at 3:15 p.m., 30 ME-109s swarmed in for the kill, wiping out the whole left side of the lead Group formation. Seven of our planes were shot down killing 53 of 70 men. Two of the planes were from the 369th

Squadron. Fortunately, Mel and the Haywood crew made it back to base okay. Returning planes brought back many wounded airmen. This was extremely costly mission for the 306th and the worst during 'Big Week'. It was a very sad day for the whole Group. Any loss is bad enough but to lose seven crews in one day is shocking. Morale took a temporary beating too. Everyone in the Group was affected by the loss of close personal friends on that disastrous mission.

The crews got a break on 23 February courtesy of the English weather; all Groups were grounded. But the next day the Group headed back to their old dreaded target, Schweinfurt. The 369th Squadron did not fly this mission. A few months earlier, on 14 October 1943, the target was the ball bearing plant at Schweinfurt. Somewhere between the Rhine River and the target the P-47 fighter escort left our bombers and 300 enemy aircraft composed of FW-190s, ME-109s, ME-110s, and JU-88s immediately attacked the formation. The First Air Division lost **60** planes including 10 of 15 from the 306th. We called it 'Black Thursday'. It was understandable why our men were apprehensive about another trip to Schweinfurt. No flak was experienced along the route, except at the target. This was attributed to the expert navigation of Major James S. Cheney who made the military his career, retiring as a major general. Prior to reaching the target, the fighter escort disappeared over Bingen. Approximately 30 yellow-nosed ME-109s jumped the formation in head on attacks shooting down two of our B-17s one from the 367th and the other from the 423rd. Gunners of the 306th claimed four enemy aircraft destroyed.

In order to complete 'Big Week' there was no rest for the weary. It was my fifth mission and we bombed the ME 410 assembly plant at Augsburg, deep in Southern Germany, almost to Switzerland. Our aircraft carried a bomb bay full of leaflets. There were thousands of them.

We also dropped chaff for seven minutes around the target. Mel, flying with Lt. Haywood, was again in our formation; separated from us by only one plane. Our fighter escort to the target was spotty with large gaps. During that time we were unprotected. When our formation emerged from the accurate but unexpected Saarbrucken ack ack gunfire about 12:10 p.m., and before it could reform, we were surprised by two sudden diving attacks, perfectly executed by a pair of ME-109s working together out of the sun. Each attack destroyed one of our bombers. At 12:25 p.m. a third attack downed another one of our bombers. Enemy fighters were always within sight from the first attack to the target. These were the only attacks on our Group and were made by relatively few aircraft. The majority of the 50 or so enemy fighters were apparently content to attack stragglers. Several crews commented on the unusually large number of B-17 stragglers on this mission. P-38s were picked up at 1:30 p.m. shortly before the target and took care of some of the ME-110's. P-47's joined us at 2 p.m. and Spitfires were met as briefed. Our gunners claimed five enemy aircraft shot down. The rest of the Group returned with flak damage, including us. It would take a lot of work and time to repair the planes. Everyone was overjoyed this mission was over. We sensed we had participated in something important.

30. LUCKY PIERRE—ANOTHER MILK RUN

My sixth mission on 28 February was to Pas de Calais, the enemy rocket coast of France. We flew 'Tail End Charlie' (last plane in squadron formation making it easier for enemy planes to pick off) in the low squadron. Mel flew with Haywood's crew just ahead of us at one o-clock. After the previous deep penetrations into Germany it was a well-deserved break to fly a 'milk run'. We blasted our target, rocket gun installations, at a little over 11,000 feet. There were no enemy fighters and very little flak. The expert ack ack gunners must have been on vacation. One plane had serious flak damage and five only slight damage. All planes and crews returned safely to base after flying less than four hours. This was the kind of mission we all liked to fly but unfortunately they were few and far between. As Shakespeare wrote, "All's well that ends well."

February, the shortest month of the year had been the longest operationally for the Group. A total of 12 missions were flown setting records in number and depth of penetration into Germany. The Group suffered some heavy losses and the 369th had not been as fortunate as in the past. That month the 369th received a commendation from the Air Division Commander. I was pleased to have been promoted to Staff Sergeant in February.

A whole week passed before my next mission. We had some training but not as much as usual. I went to London on a 48-hour pass and had a most enjoyable time. Being a 'Londoner' at heart, I went there at every opportunity and visited my friends. When time was limited, I traveled the short distance into Bedford for the evening. Bedford was the county seat. My favorite place was the bar at the Swan Hotel on the Ouse River (it's still there). The hotel is located in a beautiful and quaint setting. Men from the 306th were usually there, sometimes with dates. We enjoyed having a pint of beer or two and playing darts. Occasionally, Mel and I would go into Bedford and attend dances at the Corn Exchange. There were lots of local girls so it was easy to find a dance partner. Sometime, Major Glenn Miller and his GI Orchestra, who were stationed nearby, would be featured. This was a great treat for me because his music became my favorite from the first time I heard him play in Louisville, Kentucky in the late thirties.

We usually didn't leave Bedford until the pubs closed or we'd said goodnight to a date. Taxis were in great demand and sometimes we had to wait for a while to get one back to the base. We crammed as many guys as possible into one cab to save money. We also tried to get back to the base at a reasonable hour in case we had to fly a mission the next day. Those rides back to our base were very unsettling to say the least. Most of us had our share of beer or whiskey and felt little pain as we squeezed into the taxi. Quite often I would get the same driver, Pop Fuller an old fellow who was usually fairly well smashed. He would drive along in the blackout singing, "Why Do I see Green Grass" to his heart's content. During the blackout there was only a tiny sliver of light coming out of one headlight so it was difficult to drive while sober much less in his condition. I guess the old driver put the car on automatic pilot because he never failed to get us home, whatever the weather. Maybe he should have gotten a medal for every five trips he completed. I'm sure our 'Guardian Angels' get the credit for our safe travel by taxi.

31. FRANKFURT AGAIN

After one day off I was surprised that my seventh mission on 20 March was back to Frankfurt. Remember, our intelligence people said we would never go back again because we destroyed the target. This would be my third trip! We saw enemy fighters attack the Group in front of and behind us but fortunately we were spared. We saw B-17s from other Groups shot down by FW-190s. Our fighter support was excellent. Flak at the target was very low and to the right. The crews agreed the chaff was effective against the ack ack guns. Only two aircraft suffered severe flak damage and six had slight damage. The 306th lost no aircraft. Again, Mel flew this one with Haywood's crew. This was another good mission for our crews.

32. BIG 'B'—BERLIN

The first raid over Germany by the 8th Air Force was to Wilhelmshaven on 27 January 1943. The 306th had the distinction of leading this mission, truly the 'First Bomb Group Over Germany.' After penetrating Germany we knew we would eventually attack the ultimate target, Berlin! The 8th Air Force leadership knew the Nazi capital would be the most heavily defended target we would ever face. On 3 March we attended our combat crew briefing as usual but our huge map of England and the continent now had a covered extension. After the doors were closed and the guards posted, our group intelligence officer opened the briefing by announcing the target. As the covering was gradually removed we could see our destination by following the red yarn from Thurleigh to Berlin! There were lots of gasps, sighs and a few muted swear words here and there. One navigator almost fell out of his chair; no one jumped up shouting, "send me". For the past six months planners had been working on routes, targets, and justification for such an awesome undertaking. This very important raid could now be justified. The 8th Air Force had really come of age by its sheer power and strength.

Our group of 29 aircraft took off at 8 a.m. on 3 March to bomb the target. For various reasons, five planes aborted the mission early and returned to base. Over the North Sea clouds and layers of contrail from Groups ahead of us caused the 306th to climb to 27,000 feet instead of flying the prescribed 20,000 feet as briefed. Because of this and other problems the Combat Wing leader decided to return to our base. Fighter escort met us as briefed and no enemy fighters attacked our group. There were dog-fights west of Kiel between our fighter escort and Luftwaffe fighters. We saw the breathtaking action from a front row seat! It was awesome to watch but certainly a costly price for both sides to pay. In a few horrible minutes, young men and their flying machines were gone forever.

Inaccurate and moderate flak was encountered at Heligoland on the return flight. At 11:09 a.m. our oxygen system became inoperative, so we left the Group and headed home on our own. When the Group was leaving the enemy coast at 11:25 a.m., two B-17s behind them collided and blew up. No chutes were seen. Fortunately, we saw no enemy fighters and were not hit by flak. Mel flew with Haywood as usual. Even though we were nowhere near Berlin, all of the crews were happy to receive credit for this mission simply because we flew over enemy territory and were subject to enemy flak and enemy fighters. Again there was no loss of men or planes from the 306th.

33. NOT AGAIN!

The next day, 4 March, the Group started for Berlin again. This would be three missions in three days for me and four out of the last five days. I was getting a real workout! I could hardly believe it as trouble once more developed leaving the coast of England. The 306th had 19 aircraft flying in the 40th Combat Wing (CBW) and seven aircraft, including Dowell and Haywood, flying in the high squadron of the Composite Group of the 40th CBW. Lt. Haywood had to turn around and head for Thurleigh after reaching the mouth of the Thames River estuary at 10:18 a.m. because of oxygen and hydraulic troubles and a runaway prop on number three engine. Our remaining high group of six planes became separated from the rest of the formation. Due to weather and rendezvous problems the 19 aircraft of the 306th returned to base. The 'persevering six' that flew as high squadron joined the 305th Bomb Group who picked a target of opportunity through a break in the clouds about five miles southeast of Bonn and dropped their bombs. We did not see any enemy aircraft and ack ack fire was slight and inaccurate. All of us returned to our base safe and sound.

As it turned out, I had three days off before my next mission. I don't believe I did much of anything except take it easy. I did attend a squadron briefing and along with several other airmen was presented the Air Medal for completing my first five missions. The accompanying Special Order No. 147 was dated 5 March 1944 with the standard wording in the citation which read: "For exceptionally meritorious achievement while participating in five separate bomber combat missions over enemy occupied Continental Europe. The courage, coolness and skill displayed by this Enlisted Man upon these occasions reflects great credit upon himself and the Armed Forces of the United States". Then it gave the recipients name, rank, serial number, unit, and home address in the U. S. It also stated, "by command of Major General Doolittle".

34. BRAVERY ABOVE AND BEYOND THE CALL OF DUTY

Most of us were proud to wear the Air Medal ribbon on our uniform and be recognized for having contributed something to the war effort. It was also an encouragement to those flyers yet to follow us. Further, it was a milestone for us representing 20% completion of our required 25 missions. It was an achievement and a morale booster since some crews were lost on their first mission or never reached their fifth. Some first missions were extraordinary as in the case of Sergeant Maynard 'Snuffy' Smith. He flew his first mission with Lt. L. P. Johnson to St. Nazaire, France, on 1 May 1943. The 8th Air Force had 78 planes take off that morning but only 29 bombed the target. Eleven planes aborted the mission primarily for mechanical reasons and 38 aircraft because of weather. Seven were shot down. There were 73 men missing in action, 18 wounded and two killed.

After bombing St. Nazaire the bombers made landfall at a harbor, which they thought was, England. Suddenly they were bombarded with flak of great intensity, heavy coastal artillery and other weapons of destruction. By now the helpless planes were over the harbor of Brest, the most important naval base in France...not over England. Adding to the pandemonium, 20 Luftwaffe fighters attacked the bombers. This combined action was quickly developing into a catastrophe. Johnson's plane was hit by a German fighter causing great damage and destruction to the plane. His element leader knew he was in deep trouble because the plane was on fire and not flying normally. 'Snuffy' Smith was flying as ball turret gunner and heard a terrific explosion above him. His story, as told to Andy Rooney (better known for his appearances on CBS "60 Minutes") of the military newspaper, Stars and Stripes, describes the rest of the action: "My interphone and the electrical controls to my turret went out. I hand cranked myself up and crawled out of the turret in to the ship. The first thing I saw was a sheet of flame coming out of the radio room and another fire by the tail wheel section. Suddenly, the radio operator came staggering out of the flames. He made a bee-line for the gun hatch and dived out. I glanced out and watched him hit the horizontal stabilizer, bounce off, and open his chute. By this time the right waist gunner had bailed out over his gun and the left waist gunner was trying to jump out but was stuck half in and half out of his gun hatch. I pulled him back into the ship and asked him if the heat was too much for him. All he did was stare at me and I watched him bail out of the rear door. His chute opened okay. The smoke and gas were really thick. I wrapped a sweater around my face so I could breathe, grabbed a fire extinguisher, and attacked the fire in the radio room. Glancing over my shoulder at the tail fire, I thought I saw something coming and ran back. It was (Roy H.) Gibson, the tail gunner, painfully crawling back, wounded. He had blood all over him. Looking him over I saw that he had been hit in the back and that it had probably gone through his left lung. I laid him down on his left side so the wound would not drain into his right lung, gave him a shot of morphine and made him as comfortable as possible before going back to the fires. I had just got started in this when that FW-190 came in again. I jumped for one of the waist guns and fired at him. As he swept under us, I turned to the other waist gun and let him have it from the other side. He left us for a while, so I went back to the radio room fire again. I got into the room this time and began throwing out burning debris. The fire had burned holes so large in the side of the ship that I just tossed stuff out through them. Gas from a burning extinguisher was choking me so I went back to the tail fire. I took off my chute so I could move easier. I'm glad I didn't take it off sooner, because later I found that it had stopped a .30 caliber bullet. I fired another burst with the waist guns and went back to the radio room with the last of the extinguisher fluid. When that ran out I found a water bottle and a urine can and poured these out. After that I was so mad I urinated on the fire and finally beat on it with my hands and feet until my clothes began to smolder. That FW-190 came around again and I let him have it. That time he left us for good. The fire was under control, more or less, and we were in sight of land. The pilot, Johnson, said the plane did not start to disintegrate, so I didn't even think of bailing out. He brought the plane in for a smooth landing but as he put the tail wheel down and slowed down, the fuselage began to crack at the trailing edge of the wing and finally crumpled to a standstill. It became one of three planes that day that was turned over to the 8th AF Service Command for salvage." Great heroism, truly above and beyond the call of duty, was displayed by many airmen on this fateful day to St. Nazaire. Space does not permit going into all the details of the difficulties encountered that resulted in these awards for bravery but suffice it to say each of the wounded received Purple Hearts plus the following individual awards: one Air Medal, one Distinguished Flying Cross, one British Distinguished Service Medal, and two Distinguished Service Crosses, our nation's second highest decoration for valor in face of the enemy, and 'Snuffy' Smith received our highest award, the Medal of Honor. Smith was the first enlisted man in the European Theatre to receive the nation's highest award. Secretary of War, Henry L. Stimpson flew from Washington, D. C., to Thurleigh and personally made the presentation to honor 'Snuffy' and the 306th on 15 July. VIPs included Lt. General Jacob Devers, commanding general of the European Theatre of Operations; Lt. Gen. Ira Eaker, commanding general of the 8th Air Force, and other general and field grade officers. Our 306th Group commander, Col. George Robinson, was host for the day which was the biggest event ever at Thurleigh between September 1942 and May 1945.

Snuffy's citation for the Medal of Honor reads: "For conspicuous gallantry and intrepidity in action above and beyond the call of duty. The aircraft of which Sergeant Smith was a gunner was subjected to intense enemy anti-aircraft fire and determined fighter airplane attacks while returning from a mission over enemy-occupied continental Europe on 1 May 1943. The airplane was hit several times by anti-aircraft fire and cannon shells of the fighter airplanes, two of the crew were seriously wounded, the aircraft's oxygen system was shot out, and several vital control cables severed when intense fires were ignited simultaneously in the radio compartment and waist sections. The situation became so acute that three of the crew bailed out into the comparative safety of the sea. Sergeant Smith, then on his first combat mission, elected to fight the fire himself, administered first aid to the tail gunner, manned the waist guns, and fought the intense flames alternately. The escaping oxygen fanned the fire to such intense heat that the ammunition in the radio compartment began to explode, the radio, gun mounts, and camera were melted, and the compartment completely gutted. Sergeant Smith threw the exploding ammunition overboard, fought the fire until all the fire fighting aids were exhausted, manned the workable guns until the enemy fighters were driven away, further administered first aid to his wounded comrade, and then by wrapping himself in protecting cloth, completely extinguished the fire by hand. This soldier's gallantry in action, undaunted bravery, and loyalty to his aircraft and fellow crewmembers, without regard for his own personal safety, is an inspiration to the armed forces of the United States."

35. ALMOST TO BERLIN

On 8 March, my tenth mission was once again the Erkner ball bearing works just southeast of Berlin proper. The weather was beautiful, allowing visual bombing. The strike photos showed excellent results. Flak at the target was slight but accurate and was avoided the rest of the journey because of excellent navigation. The fighter escort was close and precisely coordinated; perhaps the best yet. All 306th aircraft returned safely. This was the 'perfect' mission! The kind you dream about. Then reality raises it ugly head and you realize many B-17s in other Groups went down over the target or were lost on the way home. Some called it the 'luck of the draw'. Many a young flyer died a hero's death so every American could continue to enjoy all the freedoms of a democratic society in a nation founded upon Judeo/Christian beliefs.

36. BORING HOLES IN THE SKY

The 369th didn't fly another mission until 16 March. During the week prior to the 16th we attended our usual ground training with limited time off. We could go to Bedford for the evening, go to a movie on base, write letters, take care of personal matters, go to the Red Cross Club for coffee and doughnuts, or ride our bikes to the pub a mile or so from the base. Most of the men were single and enjoyed the company of the opposite sex. Occasionally, one of the men would get what we called a "Dear John" letter from their girl friend or wife at home stating they had found someone else and their love affair was over. The few guys who got this bad news from home took it pretty bad, especially a married man. These letters weren't exactly morale boosters for a guy performing a very hazardous duty, but fortunately the letters were few and far between.

On 16 March our high priority target was the Luftwaffe twin-engine operational and repair facility located at Landsberg, Germany. Our crew, Lt. Haywood and several others made up the low squadron of the low group. We were caught in clouds like pea soup over Paddington, England, and unable to catch up with our wing. We returned to our base around noon. This aborted mission took over three and one-half hours flying time.

Mel and I left that afternoon on a three-day pass to London and had a great time. One night we double dated with Joyce and one of her friends and went dancing at Covent Garden again. I sometimes stayed at the "Rainbow Corner" Red Cross Club at Piccadilly Circus because it was a touch of home and a great location. I always visited with Sally Elting and Jo Sippi, two of the American Red Cross girls who were always so helpful to us GIs. They did a fantastic job!

37. BIG "B" ONCE AGAIN

On 22 March I flew my second mission and fourth for the 306th to "Big B" as Berlin was now called by our guys. The 40th Combat Wing commander flew with the 306th leading the First Air Division. The flak over Berlin was intense and accurate. We were in the flak for seven minutes and the Berlin defense was regarded as the best in Europe. The flak was so thick and heavy it looked as though you could get out of the plane and walk on it. Sometimes the large black puffs of smoke from the many exploding flak shells made it momentarily difficult to see. The continuous sound of the exploding flak shells wasn't too comforting either, particularly those pieces of shrapnel that penetrated our aircraft. Every 306th aircraft was damaged with 14 of them classed as serious; we were one of them.

A scenario of what can happen is represented by pilot, Lt. Ragner Carlson, 423rd Squadron, and his crew. His plane was hit hard by flak over the target. The number 3 propeller was knocked out of line and the engine caught fire. The hydraulic system was damaged and an oxygen bottle exploded in the cockpit setting fire to the leaking hydraulic fluid, destroying most of the instruments. The plane dropped several thousand feet before it could be brought under control. From that point on Carlson and his crew set out for home alone at 115 miles per hour. Normal speed is around 150 miles per hour. In the Osnabruk area they picked up additional flak damage. At this point Carlson took rather violent evasive action and five members of the crew bailed out. This was a good example of the kinds of problems experienced by crews in combat. At altitude, with the intercom knocked out, the men in the rear of the plane had no adequate means of communication with the flight deck. Sometimes the certainty of a parachute seemed better than the uncertainty of staying with a badly damaged plane. The five men who bailed out ended up in a German prison camp.

Carlson and the remaining crewmembers continued laboriously onward, crossing part of the North Sea at 25 feet above the water. Finally, after the number two engine quit, they flew over the English coast on one engine and crash-landed in a plowed field with injuries to those aboard. The hardships of this crew were not an isolated case. Others had severe difficulties as well with crash landings and wounded crewmembers. Fortunately, every plane returned to England, some just barely making it. Mel and Lt. Haywood's crew dropped leaflets and returned to base with only slight flak damage.

It is noteworthy to mention that on the first raid to Berlin, in early March, the 8th Air Force lost 78 bombers over the target and about 40 more never made it back to their bases in England. Some blew up killing the crews. Some crewmembers bailed out of their crippled plane becoming prisoners. Others ditched in the cold waters of the North Sea and were rescued by the Navy or drowned with their crew and aircraft. As previously mentioned, during the 306th Bomb Group raid to St. Nazaire on 1 May 1943, two Distinguished Service Crosses, the nations second highest award for 'extraordinary heroism', were awarded, one posthumously to T/Sergeant Arizona Harris. The citation for Sergeant Harris read in part; "While on a combat mission over enemy-occupied Europe, the airplane in which he was serving as top turret gunner was badly damaged by enemy anti-aircraft fire and forced out of formation. A large force of enemy planes then concentrated their attacks on this lone airplane, finally driving it to a crash landing in the sea. Throughout the descent and as the airplane disappeared beneath the waves, Sergeant Harris was seen to be still firing his guns at the enemy airplanes. The dogged determination to fight against all odds and sheer bravery displayed by

Sergeant Harris upon this occasion uphold the highest traditions of the Armed Forces..."

38. LAST TIME TO FRANKFURT, FINALLY!

I flew on the "Weather Ship" on 23 March. Then on the 24th, the day before my 22nd birthday, I flew to Frankfurt on my 12th mission. This was my fourth trip there. Some called it the 'jinx' target because our bombs kept missing the vital air components plant in the city. Ack Ack fire was low and inaccurate. Once again, the Luftwaffe failed to show up but no one complained. Fighter support was evident in strength throughout our flight over the continent, which may have deterred enemy fighters from attacking our Group. Perhaps, our tight formation also gave the enemy second thoughts about attacking us. Haywood's crew with Mel didn't fly this one. Again all of our crews and planes returned home safely.

39. A TERRIBLE LOSS

On 29 March the target was the Waggum airdrome and adjacent works in Brunswick Germany. I did not fly this mission. The 306th flew high Group in the 40th Combat Wing. The 369th made up the high squadron with 7 planes, including Lt. Schuering, with whom I flew my first two missions. Mel flew with Lt. Haywood's crew. Visual bombing was briefed but cloud cover required PFF (radar); therefore, the town of Brunswick was bombed in lieu of the primary target. There was fighter support to the target with moderately accurate flak. All the planes came through it all right when, suddenly, the escort disappeared. During the twenty minutes our fighters were not there, 16 FW-190s in combat boxes of four attacked the formation. Lt. Schuering and Lt. Haywood, 369th, both completing their 25th and last mission, were attacked and knocked out of the formation. They were later finished off as they drifted behind. Lt. Schuering lost #2 engine and #3 was damaged. He could no longer keep up with the squadron. The plane was hit by flak north of Hannover and damaged so badly Lt. Schuering's only solution was to take the plane in. He made a perfect, wheels-up landing in spongy, irrigated farmland. Eight crewmembers were captured and the other two were picked up the next day. A group of civilians with rifles, shotguns, farm implements and ropes were marching the eight airmen down a road when German soldiers appeared and took them into custody. The soldiers later told them the civilians were planning to hang them all. This was a close call. I'm sure they were happier spending the rest of the war in a prison camp than the alternative.

"At approximately 1:38 p.m. I saw Lt. Haywood's plane shot out of the formation," said Lt. Robert Welter, pilot of a nearby plane. "He fell about 2,000 feet and leveled off. His #3 engine was burning and the inside of the nose was on fire. He was then attacked by two more enemy fighters." As the plane went out of sight, one to three chutes were reported seen. Actually there were four survivors: Sergeants Harold Maron, Jerome Evenson, Edgar Johnson, and Ralph Butler. The rest of the crew were killed including S/Sgt. Melvin T. Ross. Lt. Nelson Hardin, 423rd, also failed to return. He was shot down by flak over the target.

29 March was a day of sadness and grief for me, having lost my best friend. Mel had flown 17 missions. He had told me what to do with some of his personal things in case something happened to him. I told him the same thing in case I went down. When I returned home (U.S.) in July, I called Mel's family and shared with them those things about Mel, which I believed were important to them. I don't know why but one doesn't expect this to happen to your best friend or others like Lt. Hayward, who got it on his last mission. The war gave me my best friend and the war took away my best friend. It is noteworthy that these two planes were the only two from the Group lost due to enemy fighters throughout the month of March.

40. NOT MORE MISSIONS!

The long-rumored increase in the tour of combat duty from 25 to 30 missions was confirmed this month. Some of us old timers were not required to do a total of 30 missions. Credit was given toward 30 missions based upon the number of missions previously flown. I was credited with four (unflown) missions by the stroke of a pen. Also, was promoted to T/Sgt. (Technical Sergeant) on 15 March, which pleased me very much, especially the increase in pay. I was awarded an Oak Leaf Cluster to my Air Medal in lieu of another one. I was truly beginning to feel like a veteran.

Life on the base was routine with the usual training, visits to the Red Cross girls for coffee and doughnuts, payday gambling in the squadron combat room (mostly blackjack), and seeing a movie or two. Occasionally I'd buy a couple of farmer's eggs at premium prices, which were a real treat. Trying to stay warm and stave off the cold rain and wind as I made my way around the base became a full-time endeavor. From time to time Italian prisoners of war from a nearby camp would wander through our barracks selling beautiful ornate Zippo lighters. They had somehow embellished them by adding silver molding in various attractive designs. These guys were friendly and very happy, understandably so with no more fighting for them, three square meals a day and a roof over their head. Maybe they were the fortunate ones.

From time to time, the Land Army Girls worked the nearby farms. The British government created the Land Army during the war whereby the men could be freed for military duty and the girls could work on the farms. This was desperately needed since there was such a shortage of food. These girls came from all walks of life. I dated a cute one who worked on a local farm nearby. It was convenient for me to hop on my bike and see her where the haystacks began or meet at a nearby pub. The quaint, historic pub was reputed to have been built over 900 years ago. I had to duck my five foot ten inch frame to go through the door.

April 17, 1944

Dear Mother,

Received your letter of April 10th just now and so glad to hear from you but so sorry to hear that you have been ill again and do hope and pray that you will soon recover and never be bothered again for you have had a great deal more than your share of sickness.

I'm glad Pat received the check okay and sorry it was late but circumstances prevented me from getting it there sooner.

I was on leave over Easter and enjoyed myself very much in London and saw Joyce as usual.

I was promoted to Technical Sergeant on April 10 and that is the limit to my advancement. There aren't any higher ratings for flying personnel. The next time I go to London I'll have some more pictures made and I'll have my ribbons on (Air Medal & Oak Leaf Cluster, E.T.O. with Bronze Star, and the Canadian ribbon.)

In several weeks I shall start sending some money home and would like for you to start a bank account for me.

You should receive my pictures from Mrs. Ross in two or three weeks. I loved Mel like a brother but now he is gone. Please don't say anything about it to his family.
Thats all for now so will say so long for now.
Lots of Love.
Jack

41. TWO EASY ONES IN A ROW

Early April in England was marked by bad weather. Our crew hadn't flown a mission for over three weeks when once again, on 18 April; we were headed for Berlin, my third trip there. I hoped Berlin didn't become habit forming like Frankfurt. The target was the Templehof Airdrome and HE-177 aircraft assembly plant. This was a surprisingly easy mission for our Group. We didn't see any enemy fighters and the ack ack fire at the target was meager to moderate. Only our plane and one other received slight flak damage. All planes and crews returned safely to our base.

After a day off, on 20 April, we flew a 'milk run' mission to Northwest France and bombed a No Ball target, which de-coded meant a German V-1/V-2 Rocket Launcher Site. The British called them buzz bombs. The total flying time was three hours and thirty minutes. All planes and crews returned home without a scratch. The next day the newspaper headlines read, "2,000 Allied Planes Pound France from Calais to Cherbourg". The article continued, "Adolph Hitler's Atlantic Wall took its heaviest pounding of the war yesterday as the Allied invasion command sent more than 2,000 U. S. and Allied fighters and bombers across the English Channel in an afternoon blitz of unprecedented strength...etc."

42. THE RIGHT CHOICE

About halfway through our tour of combat missions, crews were given a seven-day rest and recuperation (R&R) leave, more commonly called, 'Flak Leave'. At this point, most crewmembers experienced 'combat fatigue' and needed a well-deserved rest. Individual crewmembers could choose R&R in either Aberdeen, Scotland and truly rest or go to London and live it up. On 21 April, Lt. Dowell called the crew together to determine our departure date and destination. We could leave on either the 24th or 25th of April. If we left on the 25th and a mission was scheduled on the 24th we were eligible to fly it. Some wanted the 25th but the majority voted to leave on the 24th. What a wonderful choice that later turned out to be for our crew!

It seemed like feast or famine because on 22 April I flew my third mission in five days. This time it was to Hamm, Germany, number 15 for me. The 306th pasted our target, the great marshalling yards. We didn't see any enemy fighters but after leaving the target a nearby B-17 Group leader called for fighter support as he was attacked by one hundred German fighters. After the target, fighter support was sparse for fifteen to twenty minutes. Flak was accurate. Fifteen out of 18 aircraft were damaged, eight seriously. Fortunately, we had only slight damage. Some of the other groups were hit hard by enemy fighters and flak. Once again, the 306th did not lose any planes or crewmembers.

43. THE LUCK OF THE IRISH

On 24 April there was a mission to Oberpfaffenhofen but luckily we had our orders to depart that day on 'Flak Leave'. Pilot Lt. Kenneth Dowell, Navigator Lt. Dennis Sharkey, Engineer T/Sgt. John Mellyn and Waist Gunner S/Sgt. Harry Yamka left for Scotland to rest and take it easy for a week. The rest of the crew, Co-Pilot Charles Young, Bombardier Lt. Carl Frantz, Radio Operator T/Sgt. Jack Hubbard, Ball Turret Gunner S/Sgt. Clifford Shakespeare, Waist Gunner S/Sgt. James Cannon and Tail Gunner S/Sgt. Eugene Steinman headed for London to have a good time.

Jim Cannon and I met on the Bedford train station platform waiting for the next train to London. As the train came to a stop we entered the compartment directly in front of us. As I opened the door no one was sitting on the seat to my left. I never looked to the right. I placed my B-4 bag (GI suitcase) on the luggage rack above the seat and sat down. I closed my eyes, hoping to have a little nap since the past few days had been rather hectic. After storing his B-4 bag, Jim sat next to me. I didn't notice the other person sitting across from me. We were the only ones in the compartment. The train had hardly pulled out of the station when Jim introduced himself to the other person. She introduced herself to him and the conversation began. She had a mellow voice, which was soothing to my ears. I soon realized Jim would talk all of the way to London and sleep was out of the question. I opened my eyes and saw a dream. She was gorgeous! Black hair and sparkling blue eyes with perfectly formed full lips. It was exciting just to look at her. She made me feel warm and tingly all over. Her name was Marie and she was about my age. She was an American wearing an American Red Cross uniform and worked at one of the London Red Cross Clubs for officers. Jim was trying his best to make a good impression on Marie so I didn't say much during the train ride.

We arrived in London around 6 P.M. and it was drizzling rain. Taxis were hard to get at that busy hour. I suggested we share one and Marie agreed. When I saw her stand up I realized there must be a perfect figure inside that trim and snug fitting uniform. As the taxi left the train station, I invited her to have dinner with Jim and me. After some hesitation, Marie said she would be delighted. I asked if she had a favorite place. She recommended Genarros, a high-class Italian restaurant in London's Soho district. Jim liked to drink so I encouraged him to enjoy himself. Marie had little to drink, as did I. I wasn't going to botch up what I thought was a promising romance by drinking too much. We enjoyed dinner and our delightful conversation revealed a lot about ourselves. She was a very intelligent, well-educated young lady. Coupled with her stunning beauty, she possessed an unusual combination of attributes. Marie and I seemed to be on the same wave length and really hit it off together. I felt like pinching myself to make sure this was really happening to me. Her father was a Commander in the U.S. Navy, serving as a flyer in the Pacific Theater of Operations and she was concerned about his well being. She had a warm heart for flyers. Lucky me! After a lovely dinner in a charming atmosphere I felt really great. Jim had become a bit tipsy and ready to check into the Rainbow Corner Red Cross Club for a good night's sleep. I was only too happy to take him there and continue the evening with Marie. We had a fantastic night together! The next day I was aglow with contentment—a sensational feeling of fulfillment. It was not only the beginning of a sizzling romance but also what later became a deep love that people only experience once or twice in a lifetime.

I couldn't get Marie off my mind. I had six days left on my leave and wanted to spend every minute with her.

It was not to be. Marie worked at the Red Cross Club for three nights. Unfortunately, she had a few other duties during the day. We somehow managed to see each other at every available opportunity. Each moment with her was a precious time together. We seemed to be a perfect match. I couldn't have been happier.

During my stay in London when not with Marie, I visited my old friend Harry Bolger at the Universal Brasserie. We had a good time talking about old times and mutual friends. Especially about what happened to them since we last saw each other.

I visited my dear friends, Mrs. Dexter and Mrs. Baxter, at the American Eagle Club. I enjoyed my time with them. They always treated me like a son and I appreciated their love and concern for me. These ladies did a magnificent job providing Americans serving with Allied Military Forces a home away from home, a touch of Americana. I will always be grateful for their "servants' hearts" and the kindness they expressed to each and every serviceman, regardless of rank or service affiliation.

One day I went to the 32nd Military Police Company and had lunch with some of my old buddies. It was good to catch up with them and find out what interesting things were going on in their lives. This was an enjoyable time for me. I must admit, as a young man, I had another motive for going there. It was both pride and boastfulness on my part. I just had to show off my wings, Air Medal and rank, primarily the rank. As T/Sgt., I outranked everyone except the First Sergeant. Momentarily, it made me feel good to look a couple of the Staff Sergeants in the eye who gave me a hard time when I served under them as a Private.

It was always a treat for me to talk to Sally and Jo at Rainbow Corner. They deserve much praise and credit for the great job they did, making it the number one destination for GI's in the British Isles. Their well-trained staff did a splendid job catering to the needs of the soldiers and sailors. Some Red Cross girls were British as well as most of the people who worked there.

London is a fascinating city. I enjoyed just being there. It was fun walking the streets and observing people. There were the "Buskers," people who played instruments and/or sang songs hoping you would toss a coin or two into their hat lying on the sidewalk. Often a tap dancer danced for coins. The grizzly-looking old man on the corner sold chestnuts from an open fire and did a good business. Old ladies peddled various useless things generally bought by folks who took pity on them and gave small contributions. There were Cockneys in their flamboyant clothing; the obviously well-to-do aristocrats with men in their Saville Row suits and their ladies wearing expensive gowns and jewels. Walking from Piccadilly Circus through Leicester Square to Charing Cross Road probably provided the best 'people show' in town. This was in the heart of the theatre and cinema district with restaurants, pubs, and public and private clubs everywhere. In those days I became a 'Londoner' at heart and still have many fond memories of my time there. I guess I'll always be a 'Londoner'.

44. GOOD TIMES DON'T LAST FOREVER

Seven days passed by in a hurry. It was time to return to Thurleigh. It was the best seven days I ever experienced. I said goodbye to Marie and reluctantly boarded the train for Bedford. While sitting in my compartment my thoughts hardly wandered from Marie. Did I have any future with her? I didn't even have a high school diploma. What could I offer her in the way of security? She had everything going for her. Why consider me in her future plans. The more I thought about it, the more discouraged I became. I tried to think of other things but always got back to the one question: Was there a future for us?

I returned to the base in the late afternoon and went to my quarters. As I entered the Nissen hut, I saw only one person, my friend Bill. He said, "Jack, you and I are the only two left here. All of the others went down." He was very emotional as he told me what had happened. I was in a state of shock. I didn't utter a word. It was difficult to fathom such a tragedy so quickly. It would take time. I couldn't believe 35 brave young men were gone forever. Some were friends. Some were new crewmembers whose faces I couldn't remember. I went out the back door of the Nissen hut unable to hold back the flood of tears. I rode my bike unsteadily to the nearby pub, had a couple of beers and tried to reconcile all that had happened. I couldn't. Not 35 men gone out of 37 I lived with just a week ago in the same quarters.

We were very fortunate making the decision to go on 'Flak Leave' the 24th of April rather than the 25th; otherwise, we might have flown this devastating mission. Twenty-five 306th aircraft bombed the air component works and adjacent airdromes at Oberpfaffenhofen. The German Luftwaffe fighter attacks were vicious during this mission and we lost 10 planes—the highest losses for the group since bombing the ball bearing plant at

Schweinfurt on 14 October 1943. Two of the planes made it to neutral Switzerland. The crews were interned as guests of the Swiss government for the duration of the war. Four 369th crews, Lt. Carroll Biggs', Lt. William James', Lt. David Ramsey's, and Lt. William Tarr's, went down under attacks near Augsburg. There were about 30 ME-109s making two passes in four waves of 15 each. About 200 enemy aircraft were up looking for a fight and found one. Fortunately, only 13 men were killed in this encounter compared to much higher losses on similar previous missions.

The returning planes of the 306th were credited with shooting down 10 enemy planes. This was little consolation and a horrible price to pay for the 10 Fortresses we lost that day. Of the 12 planes, which made it back to Thurleigh with flak damage, seven of them were classed severe. It was a very sad bunch of flyers that climbed out of their planes after flying over eight hours in extremely adverse conditions. The next day bad luck continued in the Group when Lt. Donald Schaefer's plane lost #1 engine on takeoff, stalled and crashed a little over a mile from the field, killing him and eight other crewmembers. The aircraft burned but did not explode since it was carrying propaganda leaflets instead of bombs. The sole survivor of this tragic accident was the tail gunner because the tail section separated from the fuselage. It was the only part of the plane that did not burn.

On 1 May we bombed a "No Ball" target in Northwest France. We flew lead plane in the low squadron and carried a camera. No enemy planes were seen and no ack ack encountered. This short mission was a classic milk run with all aircraft and crews returning safely to base.

During the past couple of weeks many new crews arrived replacing our losses. My squadron commander, Lt. Col. Riordan, flew back to the U.S.A. for a much deserved 30-day rest. As Lt. Riordan, he flew one of the planes on the first 306th mission. It was to Lille, France on 9 October 1942. On 13 November 1942, the British Royal Family visited Thurleigh, accompanied by Lt. Gen. Carl Spaatz, top American air officer in England, and Maj. Gen. Ira Eaker, commanding general of the 8th AF. The future Queen, Princess Elizabeth, and Princess Margaret were part of the entourage. King George VI spent most of his time talking with combat crews particularly those of Lt. Riordan, Lt. John Regan, and Captain Henry Terry. Numerous pictures were taken of Riordan and the King as they looked over the battered "Wahoo", Riordan's plane that he brought back from the 9 November raid on Lille. As in the case of Riordan, it was not unusual to receive promotions from Lieutenant to Lieutenant Colonel within two years or sooner. Several 369th Squadron Operations Officers were promoted from Lieutenant to Major within six months. In wartime promotions could come rapidly depending upon personnel losses, transfers, mission completion and the need for leadership.

45. ENOUGH IS ENOUGH

On 4 May we were off to Berlin again. Due to clouds and haze, the formation was unable to leave the English Coast at the briefed altitude. We crossed the enemy coast at 9:45 a.m. but were recalled and turned back at 10:08 a.m. No enemy aircraft were seen, however, moderate but inaccurate ack ack fire was experienced at the Dutch coast. We brought back all our bombs. There were no losses of any kind. I was thrilled to get credit for this, my 17th mission..

After a couple of days off, I was on my way to Berlin again. My fifth time! I thought, "Enough is enough!." I felt very fortunate to have survived the previous ones. Why tempt Lady Luck one more time? But since I had no choice in the matter I could only anticipate whatever the prospects might be. It was a scary feeling.

We bombed the center of the city using radar because of the 10/10th (100%) cloud cover. No enemy fighters were seen and our fighter support was good. Only three burst of flak were observed over the target until "bombs away". Then suddenly, a barrage came up over a wide area that was severe but inaccurate. Total flak damage included one aircraft, severe and eight slightly damaged. Everyone returned safely to Thurleigh.

46. TIME OUT

After my 19th mission on 8 May we got a break. Our crew didn't fly another mission for 12 days although the Group flew five. In the meantime I was awarded my second Air Medal in the form of an Oak Leaf cluster. Because of our schedules it was difficult to call Marie long-distance. From time to time we tried to call each other, sometimes successfully. It wasn't easy to get through. In fact, it was very difficult. I was happy to arrange a three-day pass to London when she had some free time. To say it was wonderful to be with her would be an understatement. One beautiful night, warmer than usual for the time of year, we went to Green Park. We spent several hours talking about many different things of mutual interest. It was difficult to determine if there was a future for us. She was committed to serve the Red Cross until the war ended and perhaps beyond. Hopefully, I should soon complete my tour of missions and return to the U. S.; therefore, it was difficult to make plans of any consequence. Perhaps, we were swept up by the circumstances of the times and thus experienced the torrid wartime romance that supposedly only happened in novels and movies. Undoubtedly, the rapidly changing events of the day dictated we live only one day at a time, being satisfied with the immense joy we shared during those fleeting moments together. During our time apart, we had to be content with just our memories. Memories of the sheer ecstasy we had shared together. Could anything ever erase the memories of two lovers who had no control over their destiny because of wartime separation?

47. BACK IN THE SADDLE AGAIN

My 20th mission was on the 20th of May to Orly, France. Our target was the hangar area, which received a good concentration of bombs. No enemy aircraft were seen and our fighter support was satisfactory. There was a lot of flak over the target but it was either too high or too low. There was a moderate flak barrage over Paris. There were 24 aircraft over the target. One received severe flak damage and two slight damage. The mission was just over five hours. It was a considerable relief after the long flights deep into the heart of Germany. All crews and planes returned to base.

On 22 May, after a day off, I flew my 21st mission to Kiel, Germany. The 306th flew 12 aircraft as low Group and six planes as lead and high elements of the Composite Group, 40th CBW. The 369th had five aircraft as the lead and high elements of the lead Group. Capt. Bruce McMahon was pilot of the lead plane and Dowell flew the number two slot. We hit our target, the Naval Arsenal and the Deutsche Werke. Ack ack fire was moderate but accurate. Fighter support was excellent and no German fighters attacked our group. ME-109s were seen climbing toward us from below but part of our P-38 escort dropped their belly tanks and dove on them as they were joined by P-51s. While over the target at 12:54 p.m., one B-17 of the Lead Group (Triangle G) received a direct flak hit and blew up. The right wing came off between #3 and #4 engines. This plane hit another in the same formation and both went down. One chute was seen from the second aircraft as it was falling in a spin with #2 engine on fire. All our planes and crews returned safely to Thurleigh.

Kiel was the last mission for Dowell, Lt. Sharkey, S/Sgt. Yamka, and S/Sgt. Shakespeare. Dowell was promoted to Captain and each of them were awarded the Distinguished Flying Cross. I was happy they completed their missions knowing they would soon be back home with their families and loved ones. On the other hand, our reliable crew was now broken up and I would once again be a replacement radio operator. I wasn't too thrilled about virtually starting all over again with perhaps a 'green' crew. Captain Dowell was an outstanding pilot; calm, cool and collected under fire. I had complete and total confidence in him after flying 19 missions as his radio operator. I was really apprehensive about making a crew change at this stage of the game.

Sunday,
May 28, 1944

Dear Mother,

Received your letter of May 21ˢᵗ. And so sorry to hear about Uncle Ben's death. I know it must have been quite a shock to you all, especially Dad. Everything is going along okay for me so far. Captain Dowell and Lt. Sharkey finished up so I guess they will soon go home. I certainly will miss them for they were really swell fellows and a darned good pilot and navigator.

In a couple of days I will be in this country 3 years which is quite a long time, in fact too long. I miss you all very much and hope that it won't be long before I'll be with you all again.

I expect to be going on pass in a few days and as usual will go to London. I hope to see my little Red Cross gal if she's not working. Its like paying a short visit to the states to go out with her. Her father is a Commander (flyer too) in the Navy and she is partial to the wings which is naturally all the better.

It must be beautiful at home this time of the year (anytime of the year for that matter) but I suppose everything has changed quite a bit in the last few years due to the war, etc.

I guess I had better close now so please give best wishes to all.

Love,

Jack

P.S. Here is Mel's family address—be careful what you say because there is no definite news yet as far as I know.

Monday
May 29, 1944
Dear Mother,

This letter is being mailed in the states by Harry Yamka one of the Waist Gunners in my crew who has finished up and is now home on furlough. (He's leaving tomorrow).

A week ago my pilot, Captain Dowell and navigator Lt. Sharkey finished up and are now on their way home.

I have 4 missions to go and then I'll be coming home. It might take 10 days or six weeks to finish up because all that is left of our crew are now spares. My engineer has 1 to go, myself 4. tail gunner 5. and the other waist gunner 7. If everything goes okay I should be home in July or August.

I'm really fine and the weather is wonderful. just like summer. I'm really sweating out seeing you—that will be a wonderful day. (I have an awful lot to tell you when I get home.)

If I land in New York I must go and see the Ross family and give them all of the details about Mel which I now know about but can't write about. I know you will understand this.

Well this is all the news of importance I know of and hope by the time you get this I will have completed my tour. Hope to see you soon.

Love,

Jack

48. IKE TAKES OVER

With the impending invasion of France the 8th Air Force now came under the direct command of Gen. Dwight Eisenhower and for some weeks served more as a tactical rather than a strategic Air Force. It was vital that airdromes, marshalling yards, bridges, and coastal batteries in France be destroyed prior to the invasion. Relatively clear weather was needed to bomb targets in France because greater accuracy was required. When clouds closed in, German targets such as oil refineries, aircraft factories and major cities were selected where radar bombing could be used.

As June approached, everyone seemed to sense the long awaited invasion was imminent. When and where, however, was still a well-guarded secret. The 306th flew missions on 2, 3, and 4 June bombing targets on the French Coast. No enemy fighters were seen and there was no ack ack fire. These missions were the ultimate Milk Runs. Unfortunately I didn't fly any of them.

---

6 June 1944 - "D-DAY"—Allied Forces, under the command of General Dwight D. Eisenhower, land on the Normandy beaches in France. The invasion of Europe begins. The U. S. military forces assembled for D-Day was the largest in military history—1.5 million American troops. After two years of planning, the English countryside was overrun with 73.5 million square feet of supplies for the invasion:

- ➤ 450,000 tons of ammunition;
- ➤ 8,000 aircraft;
- ➤ 20,000 railroad cars;
- ➤ 5,000,000 tons of supplies in all.

Despite months of intense preparation, rough seas on the English Channel postponed the invasion to almost the last possible minute. When Ike gave the final order for the transports and landing craft to head for Normandy, he told his troops, "You are about to embark upon a great crusade...Good Luck! And let us all beseech the blessing of Almighty God upon this great and noble undertaking." The U. S./Allied final victory would still be months away, but the direction was now clear as a result of what came to be known as "the longest day".

The invasion was planned for 5 June but was postponed due to bad weather. Then it happened! On 6 June, "D-Day"—the invasion of France. As I recall the first crews were alerted not long after midnight and took off at 4:30 a.m. Everyone was up and about, eager for any information regarding the invasion. I volunteered to fly any subsequent missions that day but to no avail. The 306th flew its second mission at 7:30 a.m. and third at 5:30 p.m. Some crews flew two missions that day. There were no enemy fighters or anti-aircraft fire during these three missions. If you were going to fly combat, these were the missions to fly! They couldn't have been easier. Everyone was elated that everything had gone so well.

Throughout the early part of the invasion it became increasingly evident the failure of the Luftwaffe to defend Fortress Europe was due to the prior effectiveness of the heavy bombardment groups that attacked and destroyed German targets in the daylight. Reaching and bombing their targets greatly reduced Germany's ability to effectively wage war. The 306th was awarded two 'Distinguished Unit Badges', sometimes mistakenly called 'Presidential Unit Citations', for its contribution fighting the air battles over Germany. Only 27 8th Air Force Groups were given this prestigious award. This recognition was in the form of a rectangular blue ribbon surrounded by a brass border and worn over the right breast pocket of the uniform jacket. It was very similar in size to a regular ribbon worn over the left pocket. Later, it was included with the ribbons worn over the left breast pocket.

49. THREE MISSIONS TO GO

I received some good news in June. My squadron commander asked me if I would be interested in a direct commission as a Second Lieutenant. If so, I would have to volunteer to fly another tour of combat missions. This would be a paper transaction only. After returning from a 30-day leave in the States, I would be given a direct commission as a Second Lieutenant and assigned duty as Squadron Communications Officer. I was thrilled with this turn of events and quickly accepted the offer. I had to fly three more missions before the proposal became a reality. Soon thereafter, I went to London on a three-day pass. I shared the good news with Marie. She was so thrilled I could feel the excitement radiating from her. We seemed a perfect match as we enjoyed each other to the fullest. Some call it ecstasy. They were right.

Because of Marie's schedule, I had a nice quick visit with Joyce and her parents. I could face flak and German fighters, although reluctantly, but I didn't have the courage to tell Joyce about Marie. Fortunately, we didn't discuss anything about our future together since I still had more missions to fly. It turned out this was the last time I saw Joyce and her family.

After a lengthy 22-day layoff I flew my 22nd mission to Etampes, France on 14 June. I was pleased to fly with Major Charles Flannagan, a very experienced combat flyer who was acting 369th squadron commander. I had the utmost confidence in him. The round trip flight was almost five hours in clear weather. We never saw an enemy fighter and for once, there was no anti-aircraft fire. Everyone was happy to complete this milk run.

Five days later, on 19 June, I was on my way to a 'No Ball' target in France. My pilot was Second Lt. Eldon Ralston who flew his first mission in May. This was a rookie crew and I was very thankful this was a 'No Ball' target. If past 'No Ball' missions were a good yardstick to measure by, the risk of getting into serious trouble with this crew was substantially reduced. No enemy fighters were encountered. There were a few flak bursts off the coast but none near us. I'm glad we all got back to Thurleigh safe and sound.

50. MY LAST MISSION

I was surprised to be called the next day, 20 June, to fly my last mission. I guess that was good because during the last couple of missions I had begun to think about all the "what ifs". It was common for a flyer's thinking process to reach a crescendo prior to the last mission. This is when you begin to sweat more than 'little green apples'. The prayer buildup was also on an exponential curve. I was frightened and apprehensive to say the least. But duty called and I was assigned to Second Lt. Lozltev Gribovicz's crew along with S/Sgts. Cannon and Steinman, who had been among my crewmembers with Dowell. This was their final mission too.

The target was the oil facilities in Hamburg, Germany. Due to change in winds, the Group reached the target 15 minutes early and did a 360-degree flight around Hamburg then headed for the target. No German fighter attacks were made on the 306th. One of our crews saw two ME-410s shot down by P-51s and P-38s in the target area. We had good fighter protection with P-38s through the target, P-51s in the target area and P-47s from the target heading home. There was moderate to intense barrage flak to the right of us while on our bomb run. There were smoke screens and oil fires from the bombing with some smoke reaching 20,000 feet. Also, intense and accurate anti-aircraft gunfire severely damaged the Lead and High Groups but was inaccurate on the Low Group.

The Lead Group had nine aircraft slightly damaged and two severely; the Low Group had two slightly damaged and the High Group had one aircraft with a direct hit, five severe, and seven slightly damaged. Immediately after bombs away Lt. Darrel Latham, 523rd, received a direct hit in the aircraft nose, the right inboard fuel tank, the ball turret, and the back exit door. Killed by the massive flak attack were the bombardier, radio operator, ball turret gunner, waist gunner and tail gunner. The plane went into a flat spin and the remainder of the crew bailed out. Then the plane went in to a vertical dive, exploding on impact with the ground. Some other aircraft were in distress. A B-17 from the Combat Wing behind us was hit by flak over the target and exploded before hitting the ground with no chutes seen. Messages were heard that two B-24s were going to ditch into the cold sea. Air Sea Rescue replied they would try to assist them. Another B-17 lost two engines to flak and was going down about fifteen minutes from the German Coast. And so it went.

This mission was an example of why some guys who survived were called "Flak Happy" because they were obsessed with the possible dangers of it. Leaving Hamburg, I saw smoke at high altitude from a great distance. It was the most smoke I had ever seen. I was happy to depart Hamburg with all their flak guns. There were no problems on the way home except that our bomb bay doors would not close but the pilot made a great landing. Our flak damage was light.

The total flying time for this mission was two minutes shy of eight hours. When I got out of the plane I was so happy I kissed the ground. We three old veterans from Dowell's crew congratulated each other for beating the odds. It was a million-dollar experience that I wouldn't give five cents for. We received congratulations from everyone in the 369th. This was a banner day! I wish I could adequately express my feelings at that time and the thoughts flashing through my mind. To say it was exhilarating doesn't begin to describe the situation. Most important of all were the many answered prayers. There were many happy people who shared this precious moment with me, both near and far.

A couple of days later I was awarded a third Oak Leaf Cluster to my Air Medal. My squadron Operations Officer congratulated me for finishing my tour of combat duty and receiving my fourth Air Medal. He asked me if I wanted to fly one more mission for a total of 25 so I would be qualified for the Distinguished Flying Cross. I said "No thanks", but appreciated his offer. I didn't feel it was worth risking my life for a medal, regardless of its significance. Since the DFC was usually awarded to each airman who completed 25 combat missions, it might also be considered a 'Certificate of Survival'. It took me four months and 25 days to fly 24 missions out of the 83 flown by the Group. During that period of time, 45 aircraft were lost on 25 missions out of 83 while the remaining 58 were flown without a single loss.

During World War II the 306th flew 341 combat bombing missions during a 30-month period ending on 19 April 1945. 177 planes failed to return to base following their missions. There were 738 killed on combat missions and 38 men killed in flying accidents. Additionally, there were 885 prisoners of war and 69 men interned in Sweden or Switzerland, 44 evaded capture and one escaped from a German prison camp. The 306th, known as "The Reich Wreckers," was one of the original 8th Air Force Groups formed in Savannah, Georgia, on 15 April 1942. It served longer in combat than any other Group, and was stationed at one base in England longer than any bomber or fighter Group.

51. SAYING MY GOODBYES

Now that I had finished my tour, I had little to do on base but wait for my orders to return to the U.S. Since I would be going home soon, I took a few days off and went to London to say goodbye to Marie and my friends. As I was leaving the Squadron Orderly Room en route to Bedford, one of the intelligence officers gave me something in a brown paper bag. After boarding the train I opened the bag and much to my surprise there was a box, the kind that usually hold medals. I opened it and there was the DFC with GENERAL ORDERS NUMBER 116, Dated 23 June 1944 which read in part: the DISTINGUISHED FLYING CROSS is awarded to the following named Enlisted Man, for extraordinary achievement, as set forth in citation—"Jack C. Hubbard, 10600328, Technical Sergeant, 369th Bombardment Squadron, 306th Bombardment Group (H), Army Air Forces, United States Army. For extraordinary achievement, while serving as Radio Operator of a B-17 airplane on a number of bombardment missions over enemy occupied Continental Europe. Displaying great courage and skill, Sergeant Hubbard, fighting from his gun position, has warded off many enemy attacks and has materially aided in the success of each of these missions. The courage, coolness and skill displayed by Sergeant Hubbard on all these occasions reflect the highest credit upon himself and the Armed Forces of the United States".

Since these orders were issued two days after I completed my tour I am not sure to this day whether my Operations Officer was kidding me about flying another mission or not. I like to believe he was pulling my leg. In any case, I was very pleased to have received the DFC and appreciated being recognized by my superiors. Back in those days, all recipients of the DFC received an additional two dollars a month plus an additional dollar added to their flight pay. The flight pay was equal to 50% of base pay. Every cent came in handy and three dollars bought considerably more then than it does now.

I knew when I arrived in London I wouldn't see as much of Marie as I would have liked because of her schedule. We made the most of the time we had together. Parting was difficult but knowing I would return to England in six weeks or so softened the thought of separation. I was excited about the prospects of getting a direct commission and being reunited with Marie. She was thrilled and filled with joy that I had safely completed my tour of combat missions. Getting a direct commission was frosting on the cake. Most of all we would soon be together again. Everything seemed to be coming up roses and working out just right for me.

I visited Sally and Jo at the Rainbow Corner where we celebrated the completion of my tour of missions with cake and coffee. They made me a member of the Rainbow Corner "Happy Warriors Club". This was an honor given every airman completing his tour of missions in the European Theater of Operations. This was just one more touch of class shown the troops by these American Red Cross girls. We said our farewells with tears of joy and happiness.

My friend, Harry Bolger, and I went to one of our favorite pubs, the George and Dragon, near Piccadilly Circus and lifted a few as we said our good-byes. He was really a neat guy and Irish through and through. It seemed like Irishmen operated all of the pubs in London. Some owners and their patrons had beautiful tenor voices and it was a treat for me to hear them sing "Danny Boy" and some of my other Irish favorites.

The next day I dropped by the American Eagle Club and said adieu to both Mrs. Dexter and Mrs. Blake. We had a delightful visit reminiscing about old times and the growth of the club over the years. There was a wonderful camaraderie among the Eagle Club members. Mrs.

Dexter said that many of the men wanted to stay in contact after the war. I heard from her in July 1945 stating the club's 578 members agreed to carry on under a new name, "Original Eagle". She asked if I would be the club's representative for the State of Tennessee and I accepted. After a few years it seemed to fade into obscurity because of lack of interest among the members who were scattered all over the U. S. and Canada.

Later that afternoon I went to a movie in Leicester Square, a short walk from the American Eagle Club on Charing Cross Road. About half an hour into the movie it was announced on the screen that a V-1 Rocket was en route to London. Shortly thereafter I could feel the effects of the blast. The bomb hit the Charing Cross Railroad Station, which was a few blocks away. The Germans fired rockets periodically. All of them aimed at London with only one thought in mind—terrorize the civilian population. These bombs were quite destructive to both life and property. I thought about a possible headline in the paper back home—"Flyer Completes Combat Tour and Is Killed By Buzz Bomb In London." A couple of minutes later I made a fast exit from the theatre. I went to the Rainbow Corner Red Cross Club, picked up my gear, headed for the train station, and back to Bedford. At this juncture in my life, cutting short my leave really didn't matter. Something inside me said I shouldn't take any further unnecessary risks. Several days later I received my orders for the U.S.A. I was scheduled to leave for Liverpool in a few days and ship out on a U.S. Naval vessel heading for New York. After a few frustrating attempts, I was able to get through to Marie via telephone. We said our final goodbye. It wasn't easy. Six weeks apart would seem like an eternity to us. What can you say that will ease the pain of separation for two young lovers?

52. GOING HOME!

Time passed quickly. After saying farewell to my friends and several of the squadron officers, I was on my way to Liverpool. I boarded the ship and we sailed the next day. Most of the passengers were wounded soldiers from recent action in France. There were a few 8th Air Force flyers who had completed their combat tour of duty. The next day I met the Chaplain. He asked me to help entertain the troops several hours a day. I jumped at the chance to help out. My new job was a challenge. I wound up as a disk jockey broadcasting several hours a day over the ships' loudspeaker system. It was fun doing it and the troops seemed to enjoy it. My heart went out to those brave young men with varying degrees of wounds, including amputees. Some would recover from their wounds but others never would. I was thankful to be in one piece and healthy. It is so true, but for the grace of God I could have been one of them. Those guys were the real heroes along with all of the other fine young men who lost their lives or were wounded.

The ship was larger than the 'Windsor Castle', which brought me to Scotland three years ago. It was hard to believe I had spent that much time overseas away from my family. I found out where all the real eggs went to during the war. The Navy had them. Every morning we could have as many real eggs for breakfast as we desired. The weather was beautiful and I enjoyed being on deck in the fresh air with the warm sunshine beaming down on me. After enduring all the cold and rainy English weather for such a long time, this was a particular treat for me.

After a week at sea, we approached the New York harbor and sailed past the Statue of Liberty. I was filled with happiness and tears of joy as I carefully looked at her welcoming me back home realizing I was finally back in the U.S.A. When we docked, there wasn't time to make a telephone call. Our officer in charge made sure his group of 32 returnees boarded the train for Fayetteville, North Carolina. Trains were the primary mode of transportation during the war. Almost everyone aboard was military personnel. Since all of us were going on leave in the southeastern part of the U.S., we had to process through Fort Bragg, North Carolina. We spent three days doing what could have been done in three hours. Sometimes the Army moved slower than molasses. I boarded a train for Atlanta and then a Greyhound bus to Chattanooga arriving late at night.

53. FAMILY REUNION

I had a wonderful reunion with my family. We had tears of joy and laughter as happiness reigned supreme. We ate goodies my mother had prepared for this momentous occasion and we talked until the wee hours of the morning.

My mother, stepfather, and Pat looked great. I was pleased they were enjoying good health. My parents looked much the same but my bother Pat had grown considerably. He was 14 years old. I went to church with my family and renewed old friendships. We went on picnics and shared good times together and had a lot of fun. Pat asked about my wartime exploits. I told him about some of my experiences. We also discussed a myriad of other topics of interest. One in particular was his desire that I meet his girlfriend's older sister, Eleanor. Pat raved about her beauty, great personality, and the fact that she came from a very nice family. Shortly thereafter I met her and all Pat said was true.

I learned Harry Cookston, who guarded the U. S. Embassy when I was stationed in London, now a Marine sergeant, was home on leave. We had been pals in England and it was great to see him. There were two other combat veterans on leave but very few other servicemen in Chattanooga. The younger male population had diminished considerably because of the war leaving few young men available for the female population. What a situation for a virile, 22-year-old, single male just back from overseas and touted by the media as a "war hero"! Were all these wonderful, exciting things really happening to me or was I dreaming an unbelievable dream. Along with the other returnees, I was feted at different events and truly given a hero's welcome. My dentist, Dr. Usher, insisted I use his car along with his gas coupons (gas was rationed) during my 30-day leave. Other people gave me gas coupons along with other favors. I greatly appreciated their gestures and was overwhelmed by the generosity and kindness shown me. I was keenly aware the folks at home lived 'high on the hog' compared to the British, who seemed to barely scrape by on their stingy rations in their war-torn country.

54. BACK TO THE REALITY OF WAR

Thirty days seemed to fly by in a hurry. It was time to leave home one more time. We said our good-byes, which was not easy. Certainly more difficult in wartime. I reported back to Fort Bragg. This time processing took ten days! I couldn't believe it! We must have been the first returnees they had processed. Apparently no procedures were established and we turned out to be the guinea pigs. Finally, I received orders reporting to Army Personnel and Redistribution Center, Atlantic City, New Jersey, for processing back to the 306th in England.

I enjoyed the train ride up the eastern seaboard to Atlantic City via Philadelphia. When I checked in with the people at the Army Personnel and Redistribution Center, they seemed more confused than the folks at Fort Bragg. They said I would be leaving for England in a week or so and to check back with them in five days. I couldn't believe I was assigned to live at the Ambassador Hotel on the Boardwalk. It was one of the finest hotels in Atlantic City. Lucky for me, it had been taken over by the military. I had one of the best rooms with daily maid service. In peacetime my room would have been one of the most expensive. I saw Perry Como and Henny Youngman on the same bill at the nearby Steel Pier. I enjoyed them very much. Perry Como has always been one of my favorite singers and Henny Youngman was one of the funniest comedians I'd ever seen. Many top entertainers appeared at various venues along the Boardwalk. I felt privileged to have seen them. I love music and some of the musical groups were outstanding.

I particularly enjoyed eating the fresh seafood. My favorite was a huge serving of lump crabmeat costing only 75 cents. There were many fine restaurants and I did my best to patronize as many as possible. Huge numbers of girls visited Atlantic City, especially on weekends. Many came from the nearby Philadelphia area.

I found myself in a situation that was every soldier's dream. I had no duties to perform whatsoever. I picked up my check on payday and received flying pay without flying the required minimum of four hours per month.

A week passed. I checked with the center. They had no overseas orders for me and told me to return in a week and I should be on my way. Each time I checked in I got the same story. I would leave for England the next week. Next week never came. Finally, after living the 'Life of Riley' for an incomparable seven weeks, during which time I went through a devastating hurricane, I received the bad news. Because we were winning the war in Europe, especially in the air, there was no further need for additional replacement 8th Air Force combat crewmembers. I was assigned to the Army Air Force training base in Sioux City, Iowa.

55. LIFE ON A ROLLER COASTER

My hopes of a direct commission were dashed forever. I was extremely disappointed, particularly since I had no recourse in this chain of events. The assignment to a training base was totally unexpected. I had no idea what my duty assignment would be. I left England 13 weeks ago. I had not been in touch with Marie during this time. I felt distraught. It was not possible to make a telephone call to England. I had not written to Marie based on the youthful logic that I would return to England within six weeks. I wrote to her explaining what had happened. My life was a series of peaks and valleys. I felt as if I'd been on a roller coaster ascending to an amazing height and rapidly dropping to an all time low. In due course of time I learned all mortals have the same experience, differing only in degree and frequency.

The people in Sioux City were wonderful! My assignment was lousy. I was responsible for evaluating new radio operators' proficiency while training as B-17 crewmembers. I made a couple of flights with these green crews and quickly decided this job was not in by best interests. One of the two landings I experienced was more of a controlled crash landing and the other was not much better. During my first three weeks there, several planes crashed with lives lost. This convinced me more than ever that I had the wrong job. It was very dangerous. I asked my squadron commander to help me get a transfer. Since he had completed a combat tour on B-17s with the 8th Air Force in England, we had great camaraderie. He was quite sympathetic with my plight. I told him it was too dangerous flying these training missions. Being in the same situation himself, he agreed. He helped me get a transfer. He didn't waste any time because very shortly thereafter he was gone too! This guy had a lot of pull with someone high up the chain of command. A few days after he beat me out of Sioux City,

I transferred to an Army Redistribution Center at the end of the world, Sheppard Army Air Base, Wichita Falls, Texas. The only good thing I recall about this base was the fact that I attended a wonderful concert featuring Stan Kenton and his Orchestra. The music was great and I became an avid fan of his.

The roller coaster was now gathering speed. It started going up and my luck with it. I was surprised I could choose, in order of preference, three of fifty bases in the U. S. for my next assignment. Winter was approaching so I carefully looked the list over for a warm place in the sun. There were numerous choices in the U. S. but several in California, Texas and Florida looked inviting. One base in particular intrigued me because I'd never heard of it. Boca Raton Army Airfield, Florida. It looked like a real winner and close to Miami. I picked it as my number one selection. After a week at Sheppard, I was given orders for my permanent change of station to Boca Raton Army Airfield, Florida. I couldn't believe it! I was very pleased and excited about my good luck. I departed Sheppard on 14 December 1944 with a ten-day leave in Chattanooga en route to the Sunshine State. My leave was extended a few days through Christmas. I dated Eleanor every available moment when she was not working. We fell in love. We were married the last day of my leave. My new bride later joined me in Florida. Boca Raton Army Airfield was my last assignment during World War II.

There wasn't much in Boca Raton except a general store with a gas pump and few other buildings on U. S. 1. The nearby exquisite Boca Raton Hotel and Club served as the Officers' Club and Quarters. This was the Mizner jewel of architecture. Because of the war, housing was extremely hard to find. My wife and I rented a bedroom and shared a kitchen and bath in a home located in Fort Lauderdale. I believe the population was about 28,000. The area was beautiful with canals throughout the city.

Beachfront property sold for about $75.00 a front foot. No one was interested in buying it due to the insects, particularly mosquitoes.

Eleanor and I didn't own a car because a car, old or new, was next to impossible to buy. We couldn't afford one anyway. I did what most married soldiers did. I paid a car owner for the round trip to the base.

Boca Raton Army Airfield was a large training base for B-17 and B-24 crews. B-17's were assigned to the North Ramp and B-24's to the South Ramp. Since I was a B-17 combat veteran and had never flown on a B-24, didn't it make sense to assign me as a B-24 radio operator instructor? This was typical of how screwed up the Army was in those days. After several hair-raising flights with these 'green' crews scaring the daylight out of me, I asked for a transfer to the North Ramp. My request was granted immediately after one visit to the base psychiatrist. I rarely ever flew because of the large number of combat returnees being assigned to the base.

Much construction was in progress throughout the base. I got a job driving a dump truck for 50 cents an hour. This was a good deal because I hauled dirt from one location to another during normal duty hours. I could use the extra money, since our first child was due in December 1945.

----

8 May 1945—Germany Surrenders unconditionally to the Allied Armed Forces. General Walter B. Smith, General of the Army, Dwight D. Eisenhower's Chief of Staff, represented the U.S.

----

56. BRIEF TIME AS A CIVILIAN

In May 1945 the Army announced some personnel would be separated from the service prior to the war's end based upon a 'point' system. Points were given for years in the military, months served overseas, time spent in combat, medals received for combat action, etc. I had 254 points and on 15 July 1945 was among the first to be discharged. In early June, Pan American Airways came to Boca Raton Army Airfield recruiting pilots, navigators, engineers, and radio operators. I was hired the day after I was discharged at Camp Blanding, Florida, reporting to Pan American Airways headquarters in Miami.

Fortunately, Eleanor and I had previously rented a bedroom with kitchen privileges on S.W. 29th Road in Miami. It was a beautiful home and a lovely lady rented it to us. Her husband was an architect and a Captain in the army overseas.

August 1945—The Japanese surrendered unconditionally to General of the Army, Douglas MacArthur, representing the Allied Armed Forces aboard the battleship USS Missouri.

VJ Day (Victory over Japan) was quite a celebration, similar to VE Day (Victory in Europe), but with one big difference. The war was finally over! President Roosevelt didn't live to relish its conclusion. I was in Florida when he passed away at Warm Springs, Georgia. I was stunned at his loss at such a critical time, wondering how the world would be carved up after the final victory over Japan. Prime Minister Winston Churchill was soon turned out of office. That left President Truman and Britain's Prime Minister Clement Atlee. They were totally unprepared to negotiate the peace with the cunning and untrustworthy Joseph Stalin, dictator of the USSR and

Chairman of the Communist Party. The future of Europe was at stake. Did we win the battlefield victory but lose the ensuring peace? I believe we lost the peace.

57. AFTER THE WAR

After the war, my mother received a letter from Joyce's mother. Joyce married an American serviceman and was living in the eastern part of the U. S. He was a lucky guy to get such a lovely girl. That was the last I ever heard of her.

I completed a few weeks of training at the Pan American training facility at Coconut Grove. I also took my High School GED examination and received my diploma from the Miami Evening High School. Although pleased to 'graduate' from high school, I realized I had missed an important part of my life by not completing those final two years of school on an actual campus. I often wondered what it would have been like, especially during the senior year, when so many things happen that are remembered for a lifetime. There are no reunions for the freshman and sophomore classes so I have one less memorable and pleasing experience to look forward to each year. I certainly had also attended and graduated from the 'school of hard knocks' but it wasn't the same. Those graduates don't have reunions either, which is probably a good thing for everyone.

Pan American had a government contract transporting military personnel from overseas back to the U. S. This was called the "Green Project". C-54 aircraft (DC-4 was the commercial version) were used for this purpose. As I recall, starting monthly pay for each crew position was: pilot - $1,300; co-pilot $220; navigator, engineer, and radio officer - $265. It seemed most of the pilots were vintage Pan Am pilots. The co-pilots and most of the other crewmembers were recently recruited from the military.

Several months later, Pan Am notified me the Green Project would end shortly. I was offered a job flying in the Latin American Division to South America. At the same time, the Army was recruiting former enlisted men that had not been out of the service for more than 120 days. I could reenlist at my former rank, Technical Sergeant, and get a 90-day, paid reenlistment leave (vacation). It was easy to see the handwriting on the wall. There was no future with Pan Am. Eventually, radio officers would be eliminated due to the rapid development of navigational aids (radar) and sophisticated communications systems. I would be out of a job. The Army offer was enticing. I reenlisted on 5 November 1945, beating the eligibility deadline by 10 days.

I reported to the Army Reception Center, Fort McPherson, Atlanta, Georgia, for processing back into the service. A couple of days later, the processing completed, I started my 90-day reenlistment leave. I went to Chattanooga and stayed with my family, awaiting the arrival of my very pregnant wife. In the meantime, she had departed Miami on a Greyhound bus to join me. Because of the bumpy ride, she almost immediately went into the Chattanooga Women's Clinic and gave birth six weeks early on 22 November to a beautiful daughter whom we named Cheri. We had much to be thankful for this Thanksgiving Day because both mother and baby were perfectly healthy. The next couple of months were mainly devoted to caring for Cheri with on-the-job training, learning to be successful parents.

In late summer 1946, my mother forwarded a letter to me from Marie saying she had recently married and was living in the northeastern part of the U. S. I wondered in the past if I could have been that person. With our differences, would she have considered me as her future husband? Since I had not returned to England and Marie had not heard from me during those 13 weeks, perhaps she thought I didn't love her anymore. She had written letters to me and I received a couple of them. Some letters probably were lost in the shuffle because I had

222

moved so many times. Also, mail delivery wasn't dependable during the war.

I applied for Officer Candidate School (OCS) in early 1946. On 30 December I was notified I had been accepted reporting to Lackland Air Force Base, San Antonio, Texas by 9 January 1947. I was thrilled and could hardly believe my good fortune! If rejected, I could not reapply because I would be over the age limit. I knew that somehow I had to make the best of this wonderful opportunity. During World War II, OCS was a three-month course and graduates were called "90-Day Wonders". This was the first six-month course. About 150 men reported to OCS Class 47D. I was the oldest member among the 'old timers'. Most were NCOs of different ranks. The candidates represented many different backgrounds and military units.

Having served two weeks as temporary Corps Commander, I was selected along with several other classmates to be interviewed for the permanent position during the last three months at OCS. The interviewing board was comprised of the Commanding Officer, OCS, and several of his Tactical Officers. One of the questions asked was "Why should you be selected Corps Commander". I replied, "Because no one can do the job better than me". I was selected, which made me very happy. I believe my training and tough discipline in the Canadian Army gave me an advantage over everyone else. I was proud to lead the OCS Corps during the "Army Day" and "Battle of the Flowers" parades through the streets of downtown San Antonio.

There were three prestigious awards given prior to graduation. I won the Military Award as the outstanding student. I prepared a "Guide to OCS" and received a Letter of Commendation. The other awards were for academics and sports. Maybe there should have been an award for the married men who were unable to have their wives and children with them for six very long months.

Ninety-seven of us pinned on our gold bars (Second Lieutenant) as Reserve Officers during the graduation exercise on 27 June 1947. (That was the same year the U. S. Army Air Force became a separate service, the U. S. Air Force.) It was a thrilling experience to realize I was one of the two-thirds who made it out of 150 who started OCS. Sitting in the Lackland Air Force Base Chapel listening to Major General William Kepner, a distinguished 8th Air Force leader during World War II, give the graduating address became an emotional time of remembrance. My past whizzed by in my mind. I was quite overwhelmed knowing I had overcome many difficult obstacles to become an officer in the U. S. Army! I then smiled through misty eyes with a sigh of relief. This was, indeed, a proud moment in my life; one to savor.

I had not heard from Marie since her letter in 1946 announcing her marriage. Since then, there had been no communications of any kind between us. There had always been lingering questions in my mind about the depth of our relationship. Was it just a 'wartime romance'? I didn't think so. But I wasn't sure. I saw her briefly one day in 1950. It was as if we had never parted. She looked as beautiful as ever! Maybe more so, if that were possible. Marie had a certain special glow about her. She radiated so much love for me she didn't have to verbalize it. Finally, we confirmed what we both had known all along. We dearly loved each other. Marie said she would have waited and married me if I had asked her. But time, confusion, youth, lack of communications, and the war robbed us of what might have been. It was too late to go back and try to change things. Too much had happened in our lives since our time together in London during those unpredictable and unstable war-torn years. It was time to forget the 'what ifs'! We said one last good-bye. I never saw her again.

I served nine years in the USAF Strategic Air Command (SAC). My first assignment was the 2nd Bomb Wing, Hunter Air Force Base, Savannah, Georgia. I was excited to be part of SAC, commanded by General Curtis Le May. I was the Wing Communications-Electronics Officer. Two years later, I joined the newly formed 7th air Division (SAC) in London which exercised command and control over the expanded SAC units stationed in England. This action was necessary because the Cold War was heating up.

SAC aircraft periodically flew highly classified intelligence gathering missions from United Kingdom bases into Soviet air space and return. To my knowledge they were all flown at night. These very hush-hush sorties were all monitored personally by Major General John P. McConnell, commander, 7th Air Division, along with other key headquarters personnel. On several occasions, I represented communications. Everyone shared the general's concern that our plane would be detected and possibly shot down by soviet armed forces with loss of crew and plane. Whenever detected, U. S. authorities either denied intrusion into Soviet territory or said the plane accidentally strayed off course. We knew better.

After completing my three-year tour of duty in England, I was assigned to HQ 2nd air Force, Barksdale Air Force Base (AFB) Bossier City, LA. The commander, Major General Frank Armstrong, was portrayed as Brigadier General Frank Savage in the book/movie Twelve O'clock High starring Gregory Peck. It was about the 306TH although called the ficticious 918th Bomb Group (3 x 306 = 918). My new job was virtually the same as before except at a higher level. I was primarily responsible for preparation of the communications portion of the war plans. This was serious stuff because of the increased threat posed by the USSR with the possibility of starting World War III. Maybe a nuclear holocaust. The SAC motto at the time was "Peace is Our Profession".

SAC was a major deterrent against the USSR during the Cold War. General Le May and his commanders down through the chain of command expected and demanded nothing less than the very best from each individual officer, NCO and airman. Everyone understood the seriousness of the Communist menace and our need to be totally prepared for any eventuality. Those who didn't cut the mustard were relieved of their job and usually assigned to another command. There is no doubt in my mind that SAC had the 'cream of the crop' of Air Force personnel for a number of years. They were dedicated professionals who worked diligently to attain a high degree of efficiency. I felt privileged having served in this elite command.

In 1955, a life insurance company general agent moved next door to us. We became friends and a few months later he convinced me I could be successful selling life insurance. I got permission from the Air Force and started my new part time career. As time went by my business grew rapidly. I realized the money making potential and asked I be relieved from active duty and assigned to the Air Force Reserves.

I left the Air Force on 1 September 1956. As luck would have it, the military terminated free military insurance effective 1 January 1957. During the ensuing four months, I sold over a million dollars worth of ordinary life insurance policies to military personnel. I was top salesman in my company for the year and received the "Man of the Year" award. Two years later I also started selling mutual funds for investments, which complemented the protection provided by life insurance. It was a natural combination.

In early August, 1960, the Air Force notified me I would be recalled to active duty effective 1 September reporting to Barksdale AFB for processing back into the service. Previously I had been promoted to the rank of major and, fortunately, came back on active duty as a major. I later learned over 100 Communications-Electronics staff officers were recalled because of the critical shortage of officers in my particular career field.

Within a week I was on my way to Goose Bay, Labrador, Canada, reporting to the 1932nd Squadron, Army Airways Communications System (AACS). The mission of Goose Air Force Base supported SAC bomber and air refueling tankers on temporary duty, 59th Fighter Interceptor Wing, Air Transport Command (ATC) transport aircraft and other smaller organizations such as Air Sea Rescue.

In early 1961 I was selected Project Officer for the 1961 Bob Hope Christmas Show at Goose Bay with the additional duty as Bob Hope's Personal Escort Officer. Several months prior to the show, two of Hope's key people visited "the Goose" for several days, going over the support needed for the show and cast of some 70 people. I selected 10 officers to assist me. We developed a comprehensive and detailed operational plan covering everything Hope's advance men required, making sure all of the necessary logistical support was provided. Our objective was total success even down to what might have seemed trivial items such as Hope's preference for breakfast and how it should be prepared.

Proper planning really paid off! Shortly thereafter, I received the following "Letter of Appreciation" from the commander, 4082nd Strategic Wing (SAC), Goose Bay:

1. Since the occasion of the highly successful Bob Hope Christmas Show at the Goose, General Meyer, the 45th Air Division Commander, and myself have received many letters from all levels of command, up to and including, the Secretary of the Air Force, which expressed appreciation for the extensive support rendered in connection with the Bob Hope Christmas Show.

2. As the designated escort officer for Mr. Hope and his immediate principals, you demonstrated an outstanding degree of initiative and ingenuity. You were selected for this particular assignment because of your personality and sincere desire to accomplish a difficult task such as this. Your position was one of great responsibility. I feel that you were the key man, and your constant diplomatic association with Mr. Hope insured that the show and his stay were completely successful.
3. As this key man, you may well be proud of the high degree of professionalism demonstrated by you and your outstanding accomplishment has reflected credit on yourself and all members of this organization and the entire Air Force.

Signed
S.F. Martin
Colonel, USAF
Commander

After almost two years on the 'Goose' I was assigned to Keesler Air Force Base, Mississippi, where I attended the 25-week Communications-Electronics Staff Officers Course (3011). Upon graduation in March 1963, I was assigned to the 627th Radar Squadron, Crystal Springs, Mississippi. After serving as commander, I was transferred in 1965 to the 702nd Radar Squadron, Hunter AFB, Georgia, as commander.

After completing 20 years service, I retired from the USAF on 30 September 1966 at Hunter AFB, Georgia. I was feted with a nice retirement ceremony on the tarmac in front of the troops. It was a beautiful sunny day with a slight breeze. I could feel a slight tinge of fall in the air. As Commander, 32nd Air Division, and my friend, Colonel Vic Milner pinned on my second Air Force Commendation Medal; I smiled through a few tears as we shook hands.

It was an emotional experience as thoughts raced through my mind...thoughts of where I once was...not so long ago...and how far I had come during those intervening years. Wow! What a beautiful ride it had been! God had been so good to me.

It was a tough grind completing over three years of college attending night school for 10 years. A chapter in my life had been fulfilled and was now ended. As I now reflect back on my military career I usually remember only the good things that happened, not the bad. As the famous black baseball pitcher Satchel Paige once said, "Don't look back, they may be gaining on you". Most importantly, I had cut the umbilical cord and the question now was "What does the future hold for me"? I was 44 years old and eager to make my mark in the civilian world.

I praised God for His love, grace and mercy during these exciting years of my life. I eagerly looked forward to the future, trusting Him, knowing He would continue to fulfill His plan for the rest of my life.

BOEING B-17 (FLYING FORTRESS) BOMBER
Range: 560 milesMax speed: 287 mphService ceiling: 35,000 ft.

LOCKHEED P-38 (LIGHTNING) FIGHTER
Range: 1,880 milesMax speed: 360 mphService ceiling: 44,000 ft.

NORTH AMERICAN P-51 (LIGHTNING) FIGHTER
Range: 1650 milesMax speed: 437 mph

REPUBLIC P-47 (THUNDERBOLT) FIGHTER
Range: 850 milesMax speed: 398 mphService ceiling: 30,000 ft.

SUPERMARINE MKIA (SPITFIRE) R.A.F. FIGHTER
Range: 980 milesMax speed: 408 mphService ceiling: 43,000 ft.

HAWKER MKI (HURRICANE) R.A.F. FIGHTER
Range: 920 milesMax speed: 329 mphService ceiling: 35,600 ft.

MESSERSCHMITT 109 GERMAN FIGHTER
Range: 365 milesMax speed: 452 mphService ceiling: 41,000 ft.

FOCKE-WULF 190 GERMAN FIGHTER
Range: 560 milesMax speed: 440 mphService ceiling: 32,800 ft.

HEADQUARTERS 306TH BOMBARDMENT GROUP (H)   (D-A-3)
Office of the Intelligence Officer
United States Forces

APO 557
8 May, 1944

SUBJECT: Intelligence Narrative
           MISSION: BERLIN, 8 May, 1944.

TO   : Commanding Officer, 306th Bombardment Group (H), APO 557.

1. Narrative
32 A/C of the 306th Group took off at C612 hours flying Low Group
and Lead and Low Squadrons of High Group in 40th CBW. Rendezvous and assembly
were all right. At start of climb, around C956 hours, our crews in Low Group
had great difficulty in keeping up, the leader of the Low Squadron, for
instance, reporting he had to indicate 160, and when formation levelled off,
he was indicating 170.
        A/C #943, pilot Keilt, could not keep up and jettisoned bombs NE
of Hannover to lighten load.
        A/C #505, pilot Leedy, was pulling maximum power, could not keep up,
and jettisoned at 1032 hours to lighten load.
        A/C # 148, pilot Trigg, lost an engine, not due to enemy action,
jettisoned bombs at 1035 hours, turned back and returned to base alone.
        A/C # 129, pilot McDonough, could not keep up in steep climb,
jettisoned bombs at 1041 hours to stay with formation.
        A/C # 259, pilot Smith, dropped behind at C959 hours just after
start of climb. He came back to formation, then fell behind and was never
seen again. A/C did not return to base.
        All 5 of above A/C flew in 306th Low Group.
        At 1042 hours, one A/C collided with another, taking down a third
as they fell. A/C involved were # 239, pilot Lambert, # 942, pilot Jacobs,
and # 969, pilot Schlecht. These three A/C were in High Group. Some crews
report one chute, but contrails below prevented accurate observation. Magee
A/C # 113-W, and Burgess, # 181-B, both of whom flew near the A/C involved,
agree that the following is substantially what happened: Jacobs was flying
in # 2 position of lead element, Low Squadron High Composite Group. He
originally flew # 3, but dropped back, and when he regained the formation he
found Matichka had moved into his old position, so Jacobs took over the # 2
spot. Reports agree that both Jacobs and Lambert were flying wide. At 1042
hours, with heavy persistent con-trails, making visibility difficult, Lambert
was apparently caught in prop wash and was pitched around. Lambert moved to
his left trying to avoid the prop wash, and his plane came down on top of
Jacob's ship. Lambert's left wing panel flew off, and his A/C seemed to make
a loop around the fuselage of Jacob's ship, cutting or knocking the tail
section completely off. The tail section dropped and hit the wing of the plane
in the hole, A/C # 969-F, pilot Schlecht, knocking him down, as well.
        A/C # C08, pilot Matichka was reported with formation when bombs
were away. After bombing, he left formation with no apparent trouble. He did
not return to base.
        Wing leadership was praised for the right turn off target, averaging
225 degrees magnetic, which avoided flak seen to be engaging those CBW's which

held to the briefed course. CBW was south of course for a time coming back, drawing flak from A/D at Bramsche and Rheine which were identified through clouds. Except for above, course was approximately as briefed: English Coast 0817 hours, Dutch Coast 0853 hours, target 1111 hours, Dutch Coast 1305 hours, English Coast 1343 hours. Planes landed at Base 1417 hours.

2. Fighter Opposition and Fighter Support
   No E/A encountered. At 0959 hours, North of Nienburg, crews report wing to left ahead under attack. Support left 40th CBW and went to rescue, but not before 3 B-17's were seen to go down, one exploding in air. Crews are of the opinion that the formation under attack was probably last Combat Wing of 3rd Division. Our support was better than briefed, no gaps being reported. More friendly A/C seen than briefed, the feeling being that part of the 3rd Division support was with 40th CBW.

3. A.A. Gun Fire
   Berlin: Moderate, inaccurate barrage and tracking. Very low at first, but came up to altitude after 40th CBW passed over the city. Practically no A.A. gun fire until after bombs away. A few bursts in Dummer Lake area on way out.

4. Bombing
   Bombing was on PFF through 10/10ths undercast. Good pattern reported.

5. Leaflets
   No leaflets carried. Planes were loaded for French Mission.

6. Weather
   6 to 7/10ths cloud up to 10 degrees East, then practically solid with dense, persistent contrails at altitude.

7. Observations
   Good-sized ship off Enkhuizen in Zuider Zee. Same ship seen on last two or three missions.

8. Other Aircraft In Distress
   B-17, at 1000 hours, straggler from formation ahead, seen making slow circles with chutes coming out, then later seen in spin. 6 or 7 chutes were seen. See: Paragraph 2 above, 3 B-17's hit near Nienburg.

9. A/C Returning Early, Not Dispatched
   A/C #444-Y and #836-P, spares, turned back at 52°40'N x 03°08'E at 0834 hours. Each A/C brought back 10 x 500 M43's.

JOHN A. BAIRNSFATHER,
Major,   AC,
Group S-2.

235

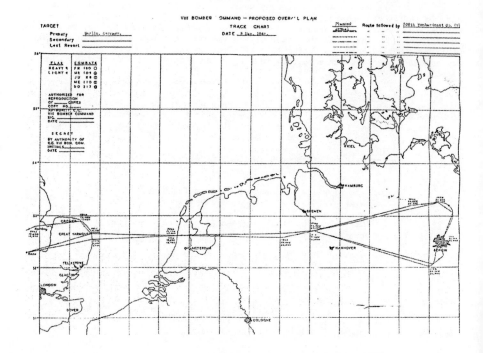

NARRATIVE SECTION "B" ⌐

8 MAY 1944

PRIORITY

TO: C. G. 1st BOMB DIVISION

M-109-D

40th COMBAT WING

ATTENTION: A-2

1. No leaflets. Planes loaded for French mission.

2. Bombing on PFF thru 10/10 undercast. Good pattern reported. .
Crews feel they were well over town judging by ETA and flak.

3. No e/a encountered. At 0959, north of Nienburg, crews report wing
to left ahead under attack. Support left 40th and went to rescue, but not
before 3 B-17's were seen to go down, one exploding in air. Crews are of the
opinion that the formation under attack was probably last Combat Wing of 3rd
Division. Our support was better than briefed, no gaps being reported. More
friendly a/c seen than briefed, the feeling being that part of the 3rd Division
support was with 40th.

4. Berlin: moderate, inaccurate barrage and tracking. Very low at first,
but came up to altitude after 40th passed over the city. Practically no flak
until after bombs away. A few bursts in Dummer Lake area on way out.

5. 6 to 7/10 up to 10 degrees East, then practically solid with
dense, persistent contrails at altitude.

6. Good-sized ship off Enkhuizen in Zuider Zee. Same ship seen on
last two or three missions.

7. 306th flew Low Group and Lead and Low Squadrons of high Group in
40th CBW. Rendezvous and assembly were all right. At start of climb, around .
0956, our crews in Low Group had great difficulty in keeping up, the leader of
the Low Squadron, for xxxxxix instance, reporting he had to indicate 160, and
when formation levelled off, he was indicating 170.

a. A/c 943, pilot Keilt, could not keep up and jettisoned combs NE
of Hannover to lighten load.

b. A/c 505, pilot Leedy, was pulling maximum power, could not keep up,
and jettisoned at 1032 to lighten load.

c. A/c 148, pilot Trigg, lost an engine, not due to enemy action,
jettisoned bombs at 1035, turned back and returned to base alone.

d. A/c 129, pilot McDonough, could not keep up in steep climb,
jettisoned bombs at 1011 +. .

Jack C. Hubbard

Page 2.(Continued)

~opm88himimi~

A. Leedy, a/c 505-V, 1026 hours, two B-17s in midair crash, one with letter "B" in triangle— one chute seen.

Johns, a/c 185*J, 1005 hours, no chutes from collision. One skidde d into the other, pieces hit wing of third ship, all fairly well disintegrated, but middle one more so.

Peterson, a/c 143*p, 1042 hours, 3 B-17s collided near Perleberg before target. This a/c took pictures. No chutes seen.

Shutz, a/c397-O, 1043 collision, no chutes.

Munn, a/c 737-U, SAys: at 0954 hours, 5246N-0920E, 25,000 feet, a/c with either letter"B" or "G" in a triangle and a yellow "J"(small) under the triangle, came up from below through our formation, salvoed bombs ix near a little village; our A/C 558, pilot Troup was forced out of formation and our a/c 737, pilot Munn was forced over into the lead sqdn. This strange a/c continued on up and disappeared into the con trails. A very few seconds later our three a/c were knocked down. Lt. Munn is positive this A/C caused the collision.. No chutes seen.

Troup, a/c 588-D, 1042 , 5300N- 1250E, two B-17s on left lost tails ; one on right #1 engine and left outer wing came off.

Kryxston, a/.c # 113-G, did not see actual collision but saw parts of A/C falling , and then the planes themselves.

Burgess, a/c 181-B(Compare this with Magee's report above) Story of this crew parallelled almost exactly the story told by Magee's crew. The following additional facts were reported: Tehe props of Lambert's a/c cut through the cxkix/of Jacob's pilot's cockpit ship; IAS at the time seemed to be high though the pilot and Co-P could not say just what it was. Schlecht's left wing was struck by debris and his #1 engine was also hit. Ball turret watched two a/c till out of sight in clouds and did not see any chutes. This crew thought that the prop wash that originally caused Watichka to shift over to #3 position came from " the low Group ahead".

Saunders, a/c 153-V, says : ship from low sqdn, apparently due to prop wash came xxe over, crowding # 239, hit wing of #239, and turned over so that two a/c were back to back and disintegrated, falling and hitting wing of another a.c in low sqdn. All went down.No chutes seen.

238

(Report of collision of three ~~L. J.~~ *April Louisin*

✳ Reed, a/c 939-A, states; another squadron flying above Lambert, backed down on
✳ Lambert and cut tail off. Turned over on side, went down. No chutes seen.

✳ Magee, a/c I33-W states: at IO42 hours , with heavy persistent con trails making
visibility difficult, Lambert was apparently caught in prop wash(they could not
tell whose) and was pitched around. At that time, Jacobs was flying #2 of lead element low sqdn, Composite Group. He had gone in there after dropping back, and upon
trying to regain his position, finding that Matichka(who had also been thrown out by
prop wash) had moved over to # 3 position. This had occurred before the collision.
Lambert peeled to his left trying to avoid prop wash, with Jacobs flying a bit wide.
Lambert's ship came down on top of Jacob's plane, breaking off the right wing of the
~~xxxxxxxxxxxxx(xxxxxx)~~ latter's a/c. Lambert's a/c seemed to do a circle around
the fuselage of Jacob's a/c, knocking the tail off the latter a/c. This tail hit the
right wing of the plane on the hole(Schlecht) and he too went down. No chutes seen.
Three planes with "B" in a triangle were reported flying between lead and low sqdns,
moving "all over the place", higher; lower; and generally about. (Cf. Burgess3 report)

Tripp, a/c 327-U, says: Collision 5305N-I225E, IO42 hours, two B-I7s came together

and hit a third all three came apart and went down. One chute seen, might have been

chance for others to get out.

Trigg, a/c I48-K, ball turret reports three chutes from collision craft.

Dowell, a/c I98-D, saw one ship of collision in flat spin, smoking, and flames.

Kesling, a/c 897-S, IO42 hours , saw two B-I7s going down, one without a wing, one
without tail. Did not see actual collision. No chutes seen.

McDonough, a/c I29-L, 3 B-I7s hi Group hit by A/c from left, spun down clipped

tail off one below. All three down, No chutes.

McDaniel, I55-J, IO42 hours, collision, wings and fuselage broken off and spiralled

down. No chutes, 26,000 feet.

Keilt, a/c 943-L, says: saw two a/c, believed from lo sqdn, in collision, saw three

go down, no chutes.
                    says:
Yass, a/c I80-K ~~xxxx~~ IO48 hours , low sqdn making left turn and high sqdn making

right turn, very dense con trails and poor visibility at the time; A/C # 239

(Lambert) skidded over and dropped down on A/C # 942(Jacobs)— sliced Jacob'sright

wing off as the two a/c broke away. a/c # 239(Lambert) fell on a/c # 969(Schlecht)

All three a/c broke up. No chutes seen.

Sutton, a/c# 055*n, IO43 collision, I chute, at 5258N-I2¹2E. ~~xx/xx253xxxxxxxxxxxxxf~~
~~fxxxxxxxx~~

Halson, a/c I63-N, says: 3 B-I7s composite Group crashed midair, no chutes seen.

McGuire, a/c# 099-S, didn't see collision, only saw three B-I7s going down out of

control, IO43 hours, approximately 5300N- II40E.

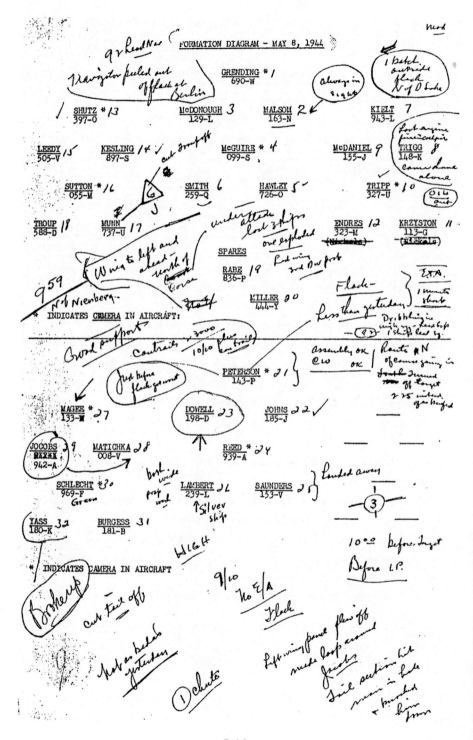

FORMATION DIAGRAM – MAY 8, 1944

INTERROGATION FORM   *23*

SQUADRON ~~367##367#~~ 369 ~~###~~ A/C Number 198 Letter D Date 8-5-44

Bomb Load 10 x 500 H.E. ~~#######~~   Position in Formation

Time Took off 0612 Time Landed *1423*
```
                        X
          X    (X)  X        X
       X     X   .X      X  X
        X       X  X      X
     X    X          X  X
        X                X
           X        Composite
```

1. HOT NEWS to be phoned in? Yes No
   Details:

   B17 tail in cloud - spun in -
   crashed - 7 chutes. 1800 hrs in way   CREW: Give Rank and Initials

   Friendly A/C in any kind of distress:
   (Give position, time, altitude, full   1st Lt. K. F. Dowell ✓   Pilot
   details)   1st Lt. C. W. Young ✓   Co-P
   Only saw one ship ? Collision   1st Lt. D. A. Sharkey ✓ Nav.
   noticed going down - in flat   2nd Lt. H. F. Jenack ✓   Bomb
   spin - Smoking flame.   T/Sgt. J. C. Hubbard ✓   Radio

                                              T/Sgt. J. E. Mellyn ✓   Top T
2. TARGET ATTACKED: S/Sgt. C. E. Shakespeare ✓ Ball T
                                              S/Sgt. H. Yamka ✓   R. Waist
   Primary   Time: *11 11*   S/Sgt. J. E. Cannon ✓   L. Waist
   Alternate   Height: *27050*   Sgt. W. A. Erickson ✓   Tail G.
   Last Resort Heading: *215 Mag*
   (circle)
   Duration Bomb Run:

3. Number of BOMBS dropped on target (all) ttisoned: Returned: Abortive:

4. Observed RESULTS OF BOMBING: (For this plane or others)

   Own Bombs: *Nothing*
                                              Any Nickels: Yes No
   Other Bombing: Number Boxes dropped
                                              Number Boxes returned
5. Any PHOTOGRAPHS taken: Yes? (No?)

6. GROUND TARGETS ATTACKED BY GUNFIRE AND RESULTS:

7. ROUTE (If different than ordered) (If ABORTIVE give time, place, height
   of turn; reason for returning early, and Disposition of bombs)
   With formation yes - 2d gun formation.

8. WEATHER: (If it affected mission) *Spotty all way - occasional*
   fingers ? broad - target completely overcast -

Jack C. Hubbard

AIRCRAFT COMBAT MISSION REPORT

8 May 1944
(DATE)

SQDN.	TYPE A/C	SERIAL NO.	FLAK	20MM	.303	50CAL FIRE	50CAL SHELL CASES			DAYS EST IN-OP
367th	B17G	42-38129	O							
"	"	42-38163	O							
"	"	42-32099					SLI			
"	"	42-31726	O							
"	"	42-97259	MIA							
"	"	42-97133	SEV							
"	"	42-38008	MIA							
"	"	42-37942	MIA							
369th	"	42-31143	SEV							
"	"	42-97181	SEV							
"	"	42-38198	O							
"	"	42-107153	O							
"	B17F	42-30939	O							
"	"	42-97239	MIA							
"	"	42-31969		MIA						
"	"	42-97181	O							
368th	"	42-31690	SEV							
"	"	42-37943	SLI							
"	"	42-38148	SEV							
"	"	42-38155	SEV							
"	"	42-97327	O							
"	"	42-32113	SLI							
"	"	42-97323	O							
SPARE "	"	42-37836	Not	USED						
423rd	"	42-97397	O							
"	"	42-31897	O							
"	"	42-97505	O							
"	"	42-107055	O			See other side			
"	"	42-31737	O							

TOTAL DAMAGED	SEVERE	SLIGHT	FLAK	20MM	.303	50Cal Fire	50Cal Shell
11	6	5	10	0	0		

242

AIRCRAFT COMBAT MISSION REPORT

SQDN.	TYPE A/C	SERIAL NO.	FLAK	20MM	.303	50CAL FIRE	50CAL SHELL CASES	(DATE)		DAYS EST IN-OP
423rd	B17G	42-97588	SLI							
"	"	42-97180	SLI							
SPARE "	"	42-31444	Not USED							
Relay Ship. 423rd	B17F	42-3061	O							

243

10. ENEMY FIGHTER OPPOSITION:

_____
(Estimated total number of E/A seen)   (Types)

_____
(Location and length of fight)

_____

_____

_____
(Tactics of E/A)

_____

_____
(Color, markings, etc. of E/A)

_____

_____

```
        C L A I M S
DESTROYED ____ 0 ____

PROBABLY ____ 0 ____

DAMAGED ____ 1 ____
(Fill out immediately
separate CLAIM FORM for
each claim.
```

_____
(Our defensive action)

_____

_____

11. FIGHTER SUPPORT *Very good support no apparent gaps.*
_____

12. OBSERVATIONS: Give TIME, PLACE, HEIGHT (List any observations of military
importance such as balloons, decoys, dummies, camouflage, smoke screens, enemy
signals; activity at airdromes, ports, water-ways, roads, railroad yards; con-
centrations of vehicles, troops, vessels; landmarks, new enemy installations,

*N/R position 52 47 - 0903   52 50 - 0930 - Couple of Scare Crows "
0954 hrs on way in.*

13. INCIDENTS TO FRIENDLY A/C: (If one of our A/C lost, state whether by A.A.,
E/A Action, Accident or Undetermined Cause) *See/report -*

_____

14. INJURIES TO CREW: (Give name, position in A/C, type of injury, how
received, PLACE and TIME.)

369TH BOMB SQUADRON, 306TH BOMB GROUP

1944 OPERATIONAL SORTIE RECORD FOR JACK HUBBARD

DATE	MISSION NUMBER	GROUP MISSION NUMBER	TARGET	FLYING TIME
Jan 29	1	103	FRANKFURT	7:30
Jan 30	2	104	BRUNSWICK	7.00
Feb 4	3	106	FRANKFURT	8:15
Feb 21	4	112	HOPSTEN	7:00
Feb 25	5	115	AUGSBURG	9:40
Feb 28	6	116	FRANCE, NO BALL *	5:00
Mar 2	7	117	FRANKFURT	8:00
Mar 3	8	118	N. W. GERMANY	7:30
Mar 4	9	119	BONN	6:25
Mar 8	10	121	BERLIN	9:20
Mar 22	11	126	BERLIN	9.30
Mar 24	12	128	FRANKFURT	7:00
Apr 18	13	135	BERLIN	8:35
Apr 20	14	137	FRANCE. NO BALL	3.45
Apr 22	15	138	HAMM	6.00
May 1	16	147	FRANCE, NO BALL	7:00
May 4	17	149	N. W. GERMANY	5:15
May 7	18	150	BERLIN	9:00
May 8	19	151	BERLIN	9:00
May 20	20	157	ORLY, FRANCE	5:45
May 22	21	158	KIEL	8:00
Jun 14	22	177	ETAMPES, FRANCE	5:30
Jun 19	23	181	FRANCE, NO BALL	4:40
Jun 20	24	182	HAMBURG	8:20

Total combat hours: 170:20

* "NO BALL" was code word for V-1 and V-2 rocket launching sites.

245

Jack C. Hubbard

ABOUT THE AUTHOR

By the time Jack Hubbard graduated from the U.S. Army Officer Candidate School in 1947, he had already proudly served five years at war in the enlisted ranks of the Canadian 12th Army Tank Battalion, 32nd Military Police Company of the U.S. Army, and the 306th Bomb Group of the U .S. Army Air Corps, flying 24 B-17 missions over Nazi Germany.

He witnessed "history in the making." Those were impressionable years that further piqued his lifelong interest in history. He pursued this field as his major at the University of Maryland. After twenty years service he retired from the Air Force.

He and his wife, Karen, live in Bradenton, Florida where they enjoy the beaches, beauty and cultural advantages of the area.

Printed in the United States
712800002B

9 781403 353726